WEAPONS
OF THE WAFFEN~SS
From small arms to tanks

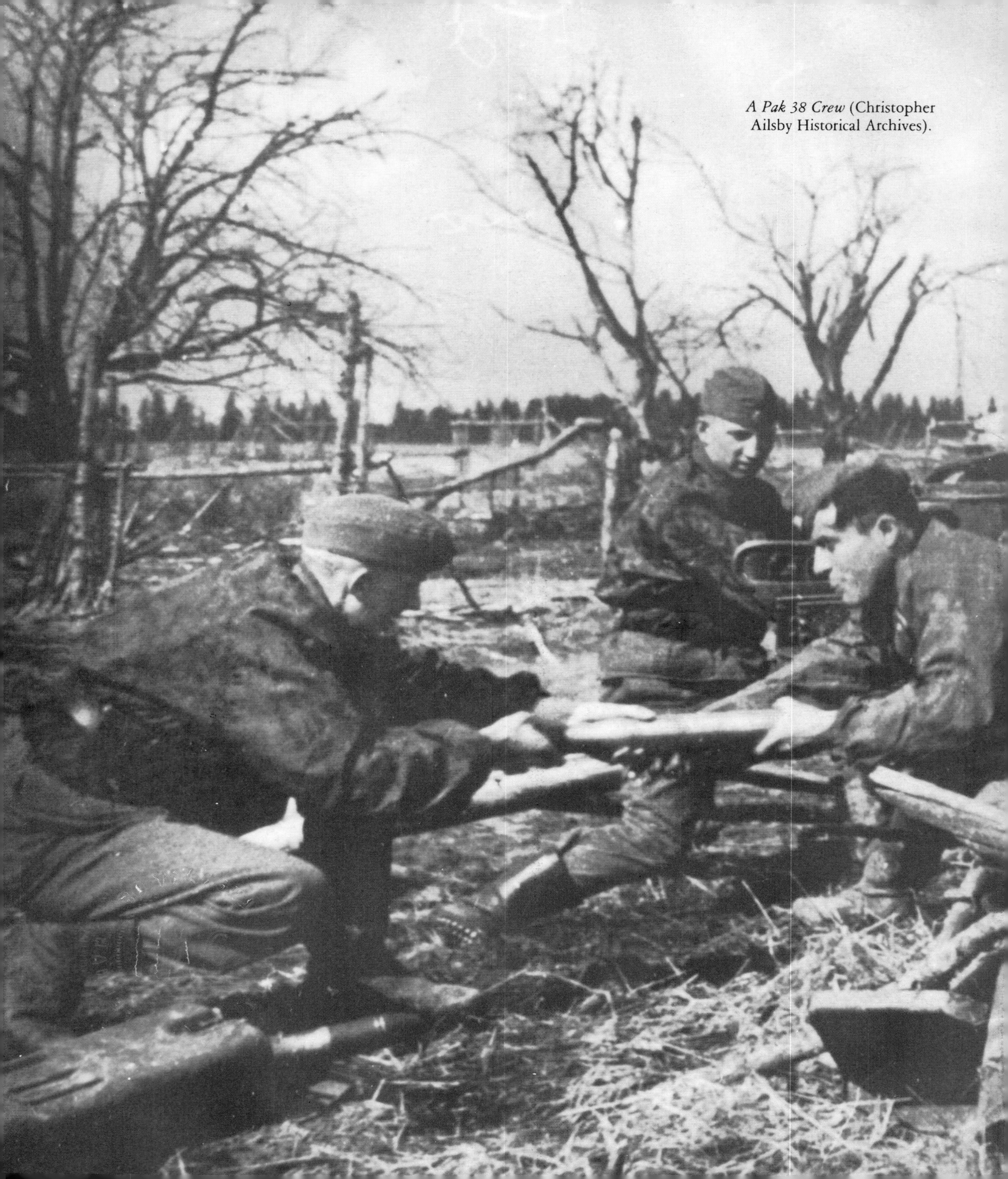

A Pak 38 Crew (Christopher Ailsby Historical Archives).

WEAPONS
OF THE WAFFEN~SS
From small arms to tanks

BRUCE QUARRIE

PSL

PATRICK STEPHENS

First published in 1988

British Library Cataloguing in Publication Data

Quarrie, Bruce, 1947-
  Weapons of the Waffen-SS.
  1. Waffenschutzstaffel—History 2. Arms and
  armour—Germany—History—20th century
  1. Title
  623.4'0943   U820.G3

ISBN 1-85260-048-9

*Patrick Stephens Limited is part of the
Thorsons Publishing Group,
Wellingborough, Northamptonshire, NN8 2RQ,
England*

Printed in Great Britain by The Bath Press, Bath, Avon
Typeset by MJL Limited, Hitchin, Hertfordshire

10 9 8 7 6 5 4 3

Front endpaper *Hitler inspects a billet of the Leibstandarte* Adolf Hitler *together with the unit's commander, 'Sepp' Dietrich, while a young NCO stands to paralysed attention* (Author's collection).

Rear endpaper *It has been said that there is no such thing as a dangerous weapon, there are just dangerous men. Hitler, Himmler and other Party officials at a pre-war rally* (Author's collection).

Contents

Introduction

The Waffen-SS led a chequered career in its search first for the right to carry arms in the face of opposition from the Army, which considered it had the sole right, then for the material with which to equip itself. Hitler's own attitude was often ambivalent. The orginal SS *Stabswache* was formed by 'Sepp' Dietrich as a Praetorian bodyguard for the Führer and carried rifles and sidearms; it would have been of little use as a bodyguard without them, and besides, the unit was so small that the Army could not consider it a threat. But as the armed branch of the SS grew in size and power, particularly after the Röhm purge and the institution of an SS Inspectorate and training schools under Paul Hausser, the Army began to pay more attention. Obstacles were put in the way of SS recruitment, as discussed in *Hitler's Samurai* (published by Patrick Stephens Ltd), and the Army refused to accept membership of the *Totenkopfverbände* as the equivalent of military service. The armed SS, not yet with the official title 'Waffen-SS', grew despite these difficulties and by 1937 comprised three fully-motorized infantry regiments, the Leibstandarte *Adolf Hitler, Deutschland* and *Germania*. Later a fourth, *Der Führer*, was raised in Austria, and the latter three regiments became the *Verfügungsdivision*, or 'special disposal' division. The Army was partially

A jovial 'Sepp' Dietrich awards the Iron Cross to some of his men following the bitter fighting around Kharkov in April 1943 (BPK/WII181).

mollified by Hitler's decree that in time of war the armed SS would fall under Wehrmacht control, and gradually the fight for arms was won, although as is discussed later the weapons received were often of foreign manufacture. This did not, of course, necessarily mean they were inferior to the products of German industry.

As the war progressed and the fighting ability of the original Waffen-SS formations proved itself even to its critics, they began to receive more modern weapons, although the later divisions, particularly second-rate formations like *Prinz Eugen* and those raised from Ukrainian and other eastern volunteers, continued to be equipped with poor quality or obsolescent weapons. By the beginning of 1943 the four premier Waffen-SS divisions — Leibstandarte *Adolf Hitler, Das Reich, Totenkopf* and *Wiking* — were recognized as at least the equal of the best Army units, and in many ways their superior in the sheer ferocity and fanaticism with which they conducted war. From this point these formations began to receive priority in the allocation of new small arms, artillery, tanks and self-propelled guns and their battalions became larger and stronger than their Army equivalents, giving rise to the myth that the Waffen-SS was better equipped than the Army, a myth which helped perpetuate much of the antagonism which had existed since the beginning between 'Himmler's private army' and the regular Army, with its proud traditions dating back to Frederick the Great (see my book *Encyclopaedia of the German Army in the 20th Century*, also pub-

lished by Patrick Stephens Ltd).

This, then, is the story of the Waffen-SS's struggle for armed independence. It begins by looking at the considerable mystique attached to its edged weapons which makes them the most collectable such items of the Second World War and which has produced a spate of replicas and outright forgeries. I am particularly indebted to Fred Stephens for his enormous help here. The second chapter is devoted to infantry small arms and support weapons, from pistols, sub-machine-guns, rifles and carbines to assault rifles, machine-guns, mortars, mines, grenades and flamethrowers. Here I particularly want to acknowledge the help of my very good friend Chris Ailsby, who not only provided information and photographs but also allowed me to examine and photograph some of the individual weapons in his own collection. (Readers are warmly recommended to Chris's own book *Combat Medals of the Third Reich*, an invaluable guide, heavily illustrated in colour, to all the combat decorations of the German Army and Waffen-SS, Navy and Air Force. This, and its sequels on Allied decorations, are also published by Patrick Stephens Ltd.) Chapter three is devoted to artillery, both towed and self-propelled but excluding assault guns and tank destroyers, which are included in chapter five on tanks and armoured fighting vehicles, while chapter four concerns armoured cars.

This volume is designed as a companion to my earlier two titles, *Hitler's Samurai*, which examines the origins of the Waffen-SS, its recruitment methods, uniforms, insignia and campaigns; and *Hitler's Teutonic Knights*, a pictorial history of the seven SS Panzer divisions. It has not been easy to compile because different sources often give different performance specifications for the same weapons. Three factors account for this. Firstly, the tiny and apparently insignificant differences which

The first Standarte of the SS, later to become the Leib-standarte Adolf Hitler, *on the steps of the Academy of Arts in Munich in 1930. 'Sepp' Dietrich is second from the left in the front row (BPK/NS28).*

Above *The original Stabswache in 1925. Julius Schreck, then its commander, is in the centre of the picture* (BPK/NS28/LoC 4032-888).

Left *The Führer did not permit side arms to be worn in his presence other than by his guards. This photo, autographed by his SS adjutant, Hauptsturmführer Otto Gunsche (on left) was taken on 21 July 1944, the day after the abortive bomb plot* (Christopher Ailsby Historical Archives).

occur between supposedly identical products of the same manufacturer; you only need to have driven two brand-new cars of the same type to understand this. Secondly, of course, manufacturers' specifications are often artificially enhanced to make their products seem more attractive on paper. Finally, some source figures are those of weapons captured and tested by the Allies, which have inevitably seen some field use and therefore suffered a certain amount of wear and tear. For these reasons I have in some instances taken an average figure for, say, muzzle velocity, rate of fire or range which may differ from figures in another book you may possess. However, I have striven to be as accurate as possible and have used 'official' German statistics wherever available.

The photographs in this book come from a variety of sources but principally the Bundesarchiv in Koblenz, now housed in a new purpose-built fortress-like building in this beautiful city at the confluence of the Rhine and Moselle. These are designated 'BA' in the captions, followed by the appropriate negative number. The second main source is the Bildarchiv Preussicher Kulturbesitz in my favourite European city, Berlin, abbreviated to 'BPK' in the captions. The third primary sources are Chris Ailsby and Fred Stephens, as mentioned above, while a few come from my own collection and out of German wartime publications. I hope you find them interesting and the text useful as a reference.

Bruce Quarrie
Wellingborough

1. Edged weapons

Within all the pomp and circumstance of the Third Reich, swords and daggers played a major role as might be expected, and alongside all the other military, paramilitary and police organizations the SS had its own special designs. The same was not true of bayonets, however, for the Waffen-SS used exactly the same patterns as the Army and the field divisions of the Luftwaffe. The principal design was the model 84/98 knife bayonet designed before the First World War for the Gewehr 98 rifle and Kar 98 carbine described in the next chapter. These were 386 mm (15.2 in) long, with straight, 252 mm (9.92 in) blades that had a runnel to facilitate their extraction, and either had plain edges or a sawtooth back. As with all German bayonets, the hilt was fashioned at the pommel to represent a rather crude, stylized eagle's head, and the grips were of wood. Examples existed with or without a flashguard down the back of the hilt. The model 98/04 was slightly different, being broader-bladed and having a curved quillon. The 98/14 was identical in style to the 84/98 but longer — overall 430 mm (16.93 in), blade 300 mm (11.81 in). Bayonets actually manufactured during the Third Reich era were shorter, overall length being 382 mm (15 in) and the blade 248 mm (9.76 in), and bakelite as well as wood was used for the grips. Blades were either of plain or Parkerized steel, that is treated with phosphoric acid and then blackened

Foreign volunteers take their SS oath, left hands on the officer's sword (Christopher Ailsby Historical Archives).

by burning off an oil coating. This turned the blades dull grey-black so they were less reflective in bright sunlight or at night, and also helped prevent rusting. Finally it should be noted that a simple spike bayonet was provided for attachment to the FG 42 paratroop assault rifle (qv).

Examples exist of SS dress bayonets with the SS runes set in a small circle on the obverse side of the grip (the side that fits into the palm of the hand), but there are more forgeries of these than genuine items, so collectors should beware. This is particularly true of examples with any form of inscription on the blade. Cords, or *troddelen*, worn with the bayonet on ceremonial occasions were red and white with the SS runes just above the tassel.

The SS dagger was conferred on all men of Scharführer rank or higher, and from 30 January, 1936 to *all* personnel who at that time had served in the SS for a minimum of three years, regardless of rank. This does not mean they were given away free — each individual had to pay for his dagger! There are two standard versions, the model 33 and the model 36. The first issue was of superior quality to the latter, and had the maker's name and mark as well as the word SOLINGEN in a circle on the reverse of the blade, close to the hilt. In addition, the 33 pattern daggers had a Roman numeral I, II or III stamped on the reverse of the crossguard, and the owner's individual SS number on the obverse. The numerals represented the three principal issuing authorities or *Abschnitte* of München, Dresden and Berlin respectively. The obverse of the blade carried the SS motto *Mein Ehre heißt Treue*

Swearing in volunteers to the Wallonien Legion in Brussels, 3 March 1943. Note the man on the right has the 98/04 pattern bayonet with curved quillon (Archiv Yad Vaschem FA-147 via BPK).

(Loyalty is my Honour) in Gothic script in three slightly different styles. The 36 pattern dagger lacked the maker's mark, *Abschnitte* number and SS number, presumably because by this time the SS organization had grown so large (188,974 men in the Allgemeine and 12,067 in the Leibstandarte and SS-VT) that personalizing the weapons was no longer a practical proposition.

The blackened wood hilt with steel crossguard and pommel was the same shape as the traditional German hunting knife. A small silver eagle clutching a swastika in a wreath was inset into the centre of the obverse, and the SS runes in a small circle at the base next to the pommel on the same side.

The 33 pattern dagger had a blued metal scabbard suspended on normal leather straps attached to metal rings at the centre and top (blancoed white when worn with the ceremonial full dress uniform by officers of the Leibstandarte *Adolf Hitler*), but the 36 pattern introduced a new chain link suspension. This consisted of flat links on which were stamped alternate SS runes and death's heads, joined together at the top by a loop-patterned clasp. Originally silver-plated, the chain suspender deteriorated in quality like everything else as the war progressed and late versions were made of nickel-plated pot metal. Similarly, the scabbard was simply painted black instead of being blued.

SS Honour daggers were also awarded to individuals for meritorious service. These had 33 or 36

A similar ceremony for men of the Leibstandarte Adolf Hitler. *Note that the man on the right has a standard issue bayonet while the one on the left has the 1904 pattern with curved quillon* (Christopher Ailsby Historical Archives).

pattern blades (with or without the maker's logo), but instead of being plain, the crossguard and pommel were intricately stamped with acorns and oak leaves and were silver-plated. For personal services rendered to himself, Himmler also authorized a dedication dagger bearing his signature and inscription on the reverse of the blade, as well as a maker's logo. The first of these were issued in 1934, a few days after the 'night of the long knives', to officers who had taken part in the Röhm putsch. Ironically, it was Röhm himself who had originated the idea of dedication daggers to both SA and SS men whom he wished to thank personally (the SS fell under the jurisdiction of the SA prior to the purge, it must be remembered). It should also be noted that the SS motto on the

obverse of the dedication dagger blade was in a slightly different position from that on the standard or Honour daggers, beginning closer to the tip of the blade.

While duelling was officially banned in the Third Reich, fencing and swordsmanship were prized skills; Heydrich, for example, was an Olympic standard fencer. Swords, and especially Honour swords, were therefore particularly valued and existed in literally scores of different patterns. The three principal designs were the NCOs', officer candidates' and officers' *degen* (straight sword) which replaced the *säbel* (sabre) in 1936. These all had a 'D' guard and a black hilt which was silver wire wrapped in the officers' and officer candidates' (leader pattern) variants. The NCOs' version

Edged weapons

Left *Men of the* Germania *Regiment in France, 1940, showing the standard Third Reich production bayonet on the Kar 98k* (Fred Stephens).

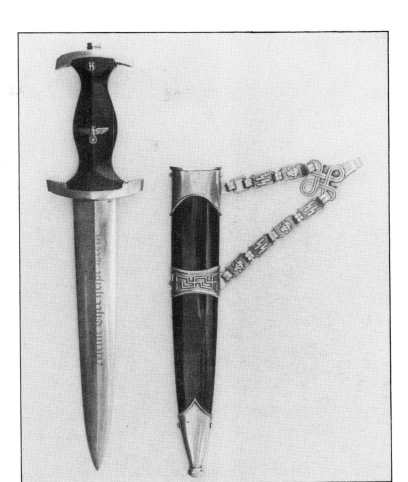

Right *A 36 pattern SS dagger complete with scabbard and chain link suspender* (Fred Stephens).

had the SS runes inscribed on the otherwise plain pommel; the officer candidates' swords had no runes at all; the officers' swords had the runes inset in a large circle on the centre of the obverse of, the hilt. The pommel on the officers' and officer candidates' (leader pattern) was decorated; that on the officer candidates' (subordinate pattern) being plain like the NCOs' version but without the runes, of course. The blades were officially plain but some swords were awarded (again, once they had been paid for) with special inscriptions, for, for example, some sporting achievement. The only exceptions were the Honour swords (*Ehrendegen*) awarded to officer candidates who graduated from Bad Tölz and Braunschweig, which had the SS motto engraved on the obverse of the blade.

According to the *Dienstallterliste* (which listed each SS man's name, rank, Party and SS number, rank and awards and decorations), only about ten per cent of those officers entitled to the Honour sword ever received one.

The earlier sabre was a much more attractive design than the rather plain SS *degen* and considerably more valued. The pommel was designed in the form of a lion's head while the backstrap and ferrule of the hilt were decorated with silver oak leaves inset with the SS runes, and the crossguard incorporated the Nazi eagle and swastika device. Honour *säbels* were also awarded prior to 1936 with the SS motto inscribed on the obverse of the blade.

One final sword must be mentioned, the Army-pattern Prinz Eugen design illustrated. This was

Edged weapons

Above *Close-ups of the hilts of the standard SS dagger (left) and Honour dagger (right)* (Fred Stephens).

Below *The inscription on the obverse of the SS dagger's blade* (Fred Stephens).

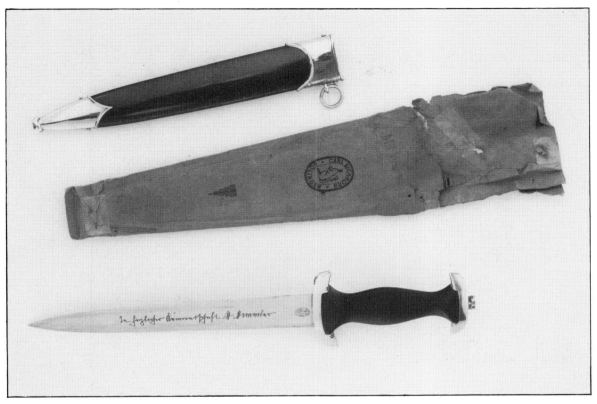

Above *A Himmler dedication dagger complete with scabbard and presentation packet (Fred Stephens).*

Below *A standard blade and a dedication blade: note the difference in the positioning of the motto (Fred Stephens).*

apparently worn exclusively within the Waffen-SS by special dispensation by officers and NCOs of the 7th SS Freiwilligen Gebirgs Division *Prinz Eugen*.

Fighting knives were also used extensively by the Waffen-SS but these were private purchase items manufactured commercially and existed in too many variations for any description to be attempted. SS paratroops, of course, used the standard *Fallschirmjäger* gravity knife.

Right *SS officers in Italy, April 1939. The officer pattern* degen *can be seen on the left and the 36 pattern dagger on the right* (Fred Stephens).

Below *Officers of the* Der Führer *Regiment wearing the straight SS* degen (Christopher Ailsby Historical Archives).

Weapons of the Waffen-SS

Edged weapons

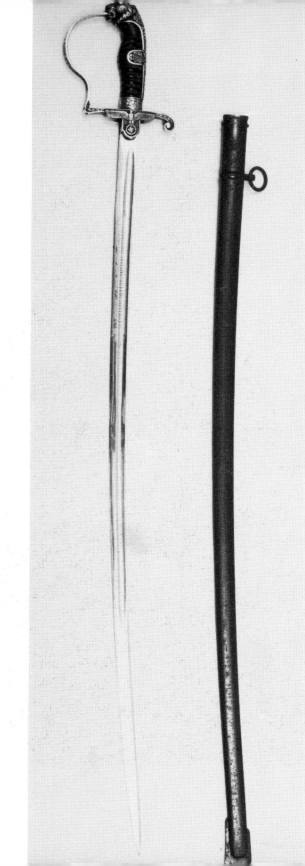

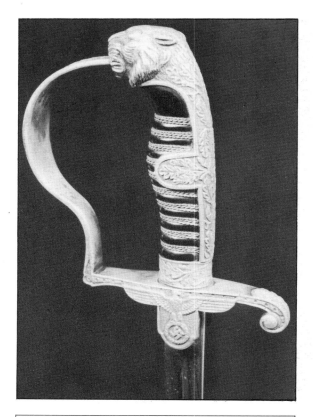

Above *Close-up of the hilt of the* säbel
(Fred Stephens).

Left *The officers'* säbel (Fred Stephens).

Weapons of the Waffen-SS

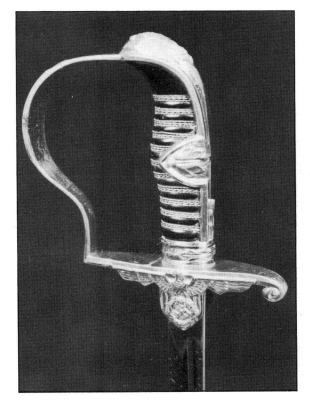

Above *Close-up of the hilt of the* Prinz Eugen *pattern sword* (Fred Stephens).

Right *A Hauptsturmführer of the* Prinz Eugen *Division wearing the sword of the same name. He has just been awarded the War Merit Cross Second Class — Bronze with Swords* (Fred Stephens).

2. Small arms

There was a greater profusion of small arms in the Second World War than during any other conflict in history and tens of thousands survive to this day, not just as war souvenirs or in the hands of collectors and museums, but also as weapons for the dozens of 'liberation' movements, for the armies of several small and impoverished nations, and for terrorists — although today the terrorist is more likely to have access to more modern arsenals. Within the German Army, and even more so in the less rigid and more individual Waffen-SS, carrying a personal weapon, particularly a pistol or sub-machine-gun (SMG), became something of a cachet. A pistol is really of little value in a combat situation, having limited range and accuracy, but being small it can be conveniently carried by the crews of tanks and other armoured fighting vehicles in their cramped interiors, as can SMGs, whereas a rifle would be too unwieldy. However, a pistol is a great morale-booster and a single man so armed can often force the surrender of several opponents if they are shocked and demoralized, as happened quite often in France and during the early period of the advance into Russia. A pistol is also a last defence against capture, and soldiers of the Waffen-SS in Russia were well aware that a 'friendly' bullet was usually preferable to surrender. Pistols and sub-machine-guns are also useful in close-quarters fighting, as when clearing a

'Broom handle' mauser being worn by a Leibstandarte NCO during the French campaign, May 1940 (Fred Stephens).

building or a trench, and in dense woods where it would be difficult to aim a longer-barrelled weapon. Pistols are symbols of authority too, and hence are worn by officers and military policemen as a standard part of their uniform.

The principal side-arms worn by German soldiers were the 9 mm P 08 Luger, the Walther P 38, PP and PPK and, after the fall of Belgium in 1940, the Fabrique Nationale (FN) Browning High Power (HP), but these only represent the tip of the iceberg. Police issue pistols, the First World War Mauser C/96 (the so-called 'broomhandle' Mauser), remained extremely popular, and captured British, French, Russian and, later, American weapons were also very widely used. In fact it would probably be fair to say that there was hardly a single pistol from any of the combatant nations which was *not* used by the Waffen-SS! However, this is not a handbook on firearms, so only the principal types will be described.

The oldest design in widespread service was the P 08 Luger, designed at the turn of the century by George Luger and taken into service first by the Swiss Army in 1900 and then by the Germans in 1908. It was originally made in 7.65 mm calibre, and a few of these survived into the Second World War, although most weapons were 9 mm Parabellums ('Parabellum' simply means 'for war' and originated as the Luger factory's telegraph codename. In German service the P 08 was commonly referred to as 'the Parabellum' but elsewhere it is popularly just called 'the Luger'. It is a recoil-operated single-shot automatic with a

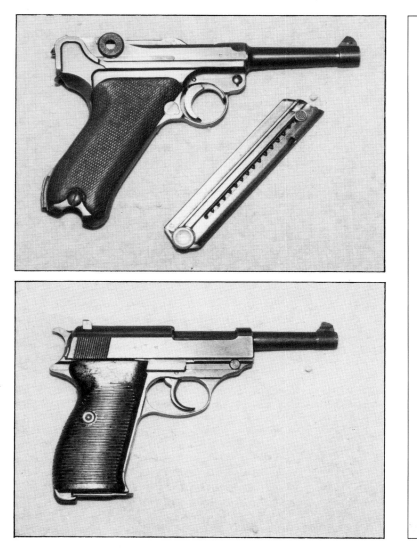

The P 08 Luger (Author photo courtesy of Christopher Ailsby).

The Walther P 38 (Author photo courtesy of Christopher Ailsby).

toggle lock and manual safety switch on the left side of the receiver. The standard barrel length is 102 mm (4 in) but versions with 152, 203 and even 250 mm (6, 8 and 10 in) barrels also exist. (A 32-round snail magazine and wooden shoulder stock were available for the longer-barrelled versions, turning them effectively into machine carbines, but these were only produced in comparatively small quantities and are today real collectors' items.) The P 08 has an inverted V blade front site and an open V notch at the rear. Eight cartridges are loaded in the sliding box magazine, the bullets weighing between 7.15 and 8.125 g (110-125 gr) being fired at a muzzle velocity of between 317 and 457 m/sec (1,040 to 1,500 ft/sec). The maximum range is some 1,100 m (1,200 yd) but of course at that distance the bullet is entirely spent and harmless. For practical purposes the maximum effective combat range (with standard 102 mm barrel) is about 70 m (75 yd), but it would normally not be used beyond about 50 m (55 yd).

Weapons of the Waffen-SS

In 1938 the P 08 began to be replaced by the Walther P 38, which was simpler and therefore less expensive to manufacture. It was and is an excellent weapon and in 1957 was actually put back into manufacture for the Bundeswehr after the Federal Republic of Germany became part of NATO. It was based on the earlier Walther PP of 7.65 mm calibre (see below), a police issue weapon, and incorporates many similar features, including a safety lock preventing accidental firing even when the manual 'on/off' switch is 'off', and an indicator to show when there is a round in the chamber. (There were self-inflicted casualties with the Luger since it was possible to strip it whilst loaded and the favoured method of reassembly involved holding the barrel against one's belt buckle in order to push it back within the recoil mechanism, with unfortunate results if the release catch on the side of the chamber was pushed.) First recipients of the P 38 were Hitler's new Panzer troops and it is such a good sidearm that Oberführer Gärtner, head of the SS Procurement Office, attempted at one point (unsuccessfully!) to divert all production for the Waffen-SS. The hand grip is positive and comfortable, the action smooth and aiming easy. The P 38 is also easier to field-strip than the P 08. It has a 124 mm (4.9 in) barrel with the same type of sights as on the Luger and takes a similar eight-round box magazine. The manufacturer claimed a combat range of 115 m (125 yd) but in reality it is half that, except in the hands of a marksman. Muzzle velocity is identical to that of the Luger.

Because demand for the P 38 rapidly outstripped supply as the German Army and Waffen-SS were expanded, the earlier PP was also taken into service in large numbers, along with the shorter-barrelled PPK which was often favoured because it could so easily be concealed. (This made it a popular weapon with the Gestapo and SD.) The PP was first introduced in 1929 and continued to be manufactured throughout the war in 6.35, 7.65 and 9 mm versions. Barrel length of the PP is 99 mm (3.9 in), of the PPK 86 mm (3.4 in). Both were of advanced design for their time, with blow-back action, external hammers, double-action triggers and positive safety features. They are also extremely easy to field-strip, which is always a combat asset. Muzzle velocity is 280 m/sec (PPK) to 290 m/sec (PP) (919-952 ft/sec) but effective range is only about 25 m (27 yd). The PP takes an eight-round box magazine, the PPK a slightly shorter one with seven cartridges.

Apart from the above two 'pocket pistols', similar weapons were produced by no fewer than 29 other German firms, all of which saw service in various quantities, usually being purchased privately. Only the Mauser and Sauer und Sohn versions were issued to the armed forces in large numbers. The 7.65 mm Mauser HSc is of a very streamlined design for ease in drawing, light in weight and comfortable to use. Of 7.65 mm calibre, it has a short barrel only 85.725 mm (3.375 in) long, approximately the same as the PPK; the Sauer was virtually the same apart from being a squarer, more conventional shape. Both utilized straightforward blow-back mechanisms, had eight-round box magazines and were otherwise virtually identical to the PP. Smaller variations of 6.35 mm calibre ('ladies' guns') were also produced.

The Mauser C/96 was first produced in 1896 and went on to be one of the most famous handguns of the twentieth century, the first real automatic pistol with a self-loading magazine. Its high velocity (433 m/sec or 1,421 ft/sec) imparts a lethal impact to either the original 7.63 mm or later 9 mm Parabellum rounds, and it can be sighted to 1,000 m (1,094 yd). Shots at this sort of range would only be attempted using the wooden stock, ingeniously crafted and hollow so that it doubles as a holster. (On some models, the stock/holster also accommodates stripping and cleaning tools.) Unlike later automatic pistols, the 'broomhandle' Mauser has a simple wooden grip (hence its name), with the magazine in front of the trigger being loaded from the top of the barrel by 10-round unboxed clips. Later, spurred on by adaptations of the basic design made under licence in Spain and China during the 1920s, Mauser introduced a revised model with a 20-round magazine capable of firing fully-automatically like a sub-machine-gun, rather than just single shot. Although of limited value as a combat weapon because firing in this mode makes the barrel rise sharply (unless it is held sideways in which case it acts like a scythe), the sharp 'brrrrp' and hail of metal tends to make opponents a little bit nervous and rather liable to dive for cover — a useful attribute. Despite the fact

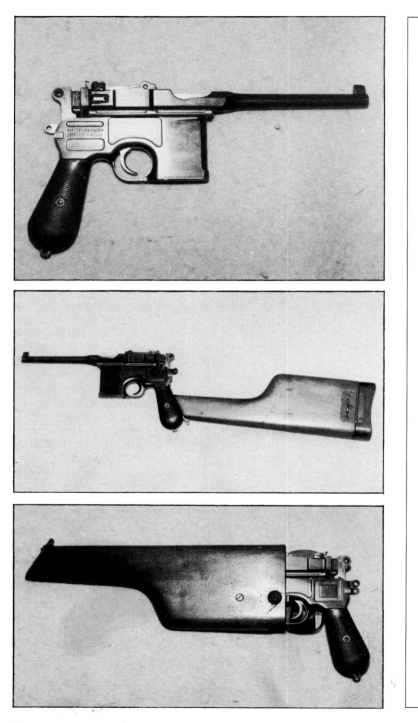

The 'broom handle' Mauser complete with wooden holster/stock (Author photos courtesy of Christopher Ailsby).

Weapons of the Waffen-SS

that it has been superseded by genuine purpose-built sub-machine-guns, the C/96 was and is a much-respected and sought-after weapon, and indeed a modified version, designated Type 80, is still produced today for export by the Chinese. Sidearms, or handguns as the Americans know them, do not date as rapidly as larger pieces of equipment, such as tanks and aircraft.

The Mauser has a barrel 140 mm (5.5 in) long, overall length being 308 mm (12.1 in), and weighs a hefty 1.22 kg (2.7 lb), making single-handed firing almost impossible. (Comparative weights of the P 08 and P38 are 0.88 kg (1.9 lb) and 0.96 kg (2.1 lb), and the Mauser's grip is hardly ergonomic...)

Last of the standard issue sidearms was the FN-made version of the Browning High Power (or, in Americanese, Hi-Power) automatic. Based on a design of 1925, its manufacture in Belgium commenced ten years later and it was kept in production by the Germans until 1944 and by the Belgians themselves ever since. More Browning HPs have probably been manufactured than any other pistol. It is a recoil-operated automatic pistol of conventional configuration with a 112 mm (4.1 in) barrel firing the same ammunition at the same muzzle velocity and with the same range as the Luger, Walther or Mauser, but has a 13-round box magazine which makes it a much more useful

weapon. (This was achieved by loading the cartridges in two staggered rows, thickening but not lengthening the butt and in fact giving a much more comfortable grip than the Luger or Mauser.) Despite this, overall weight is only fractionally higher than that of the P 08 or P38 at 1.01 kg (2.2 lb), and considerably less than that of the Mauser. It is a gun that 'feels' right, which goes a long way towards explaining its enormous popularity over more than 50 years.

Another FN pistol, the smaller 9 mm Browning Model 1910, was also kept in production throughout the war and was widely used by the Waffen-SS. It has a barrel only 89 mm (3.5 in) long and a 7-round magazine, so is most closely comparable to the Walther PPK, and indeed was similarly designed as a police rather than a military weapon. It is still in production some 80 years after it first appeared.

Czechoslovakia, as seen elsewhere in this book, became one of Europe's most prolific and inventive arms manufacturers after the country came into being at the end of the First World War, and the Germans profited greatly from this after they overran ('liberated') the country in March 1939. In the field of sidearms, strangely, though, the Czechs lagged behind developments in other countries and their principal military pistol, the 9 mm CZ 38 (which became the P 39(t) in German service) was a

SS infantry cleaning their rifles and bayonets during a lull in the fighting, France, May 1940 (BA 81/146/12a).

rather clumsy double-action design with a very heavy trigger pull which ruined accurate aiming. It was unpopular with the German forces, partly because it jammed easily, and in the Waffen-SS was used principally to equip the rather less-than-elite formations such as the Polizei Division. Barrel length was 119 mm (4.7 in), the magazine contained eight rounds and ballistic qualities were comparable to those of equivalent German 9 mm pistols.

Perhaps surprisingly, a much more modern design very similar in appearance to the FN Browning came from captured Polish stocks after the 1939 campaign. The 9 mm Radom wz 35 entered German service as the P 35(p), and the muzzle velocity, range and other characteristics were much the same as above from its 121 mm (4.76 in) barrel, and the magazine was again of the eight-round box-type. (It is very difficult to distinguish many of these automatic pistols from each other in wartime photographs.) A very much more elderly design came from occupied Denmark; the M1910/22 closely resembled the 'broom-

handle' Mauser and was of the same vintage but with a far superior grip. The interchangeable 6 or 10-round magazines were inserted from below but refilled from above the barrel unless a spare magazine was available to clip into place. Unlike the later Mausers, it did not have an automatic fire capability.

France did not contribute a great deal to the Waffen-SS armoury in terms of sidearms. Some ancient black-powder revolvers, commonly called 'Lebel', of late nineteenth-century design were perhaps picked up by enthusiasts. Designated Models 1873, 1874 and 1892, these were six-shot double-action (hammer and/or trigger) weapons of 8-11 mm calibre — quite capable of killing, of course, but (like so much of the French Army at the time) totally obsolete by 1940, even though they were standard officers' issue. An automatic, the 7.65 mm Model 1935 and 1935S, had begun to replace these museum pieces, but it lacked the modern features of the FN Browning which it closely resembled, especially in the safety features dear to the heart of any soldier who does not want a

Weapons of the Waffen-SS

firearm going off unless he is controlling it. Commandeered examples were more often thrown away than kept for combat.

One automatic pistol which was particularly popular with the Austrian officers in the *Der Führer* Regiment and other formations was the elegant Hungarian-designed Frommer 7.65 mm on which, unusually, a long recoil mechanism was used, the barrel travelling fully to the rear of the pistol. This makes firing a pleasure and accurate aiming much easier than with most other similar weapons. A penalty for this was that the magazine can only hold 7 rounds. Barrel length is 82.5 mm (3.25 in) and muzzle velocity 299 m/sec (980 ft/sec), giving an effective range of 50 m (55 yd).

A couple of Italian designs were used, notably the old Glisenti 9 mm Model 1910, a weapon superficially very similar in appearance to the P 08 Luger and of the same vintage, and the Beretta 9 mm Model 1934. The former has a seven-round magazine and its 95 mm (3.74 in) barrel imparts a muzzle velocity of 258 m/sec (846 ft/sec). It employs a locked breech mechanism. One flaw was that the designers, bearing simplified maintenance in mind, made almost the whole of the left-hand side detachable in a single piece, but this weakened the gun and in strenuous combat situations it was easily damaged. The Beretta, obviously a much more modern design, was therefore preferred. This is a blow-back type, single shot again, with a seven-round magazine, but can only accept 6 g (95 gr) bullets instead of the more normal 9 mm Parabellum size of 8 g (125 gr), so although muzzle velocity is 290 m/sec (952 ft/sec), effective range is only 25 m (27 yd).

Norwegian volunteers in the *Wiking* Division often preferred the home-grown Model 1914 11.43 mm automatic, which was a licence-built copy of the famous Colt M1911/M1911A1 0.45 in. Its heavy calibre gives the American and Norwegian weapons enormous punch, and after the Germans started meeting Americans in combat in 1943, the Colt became as much a prized war souvenir as the Luger was to the Allies. First designed at the turn of the century in response to urgent requests for a pistol with greater stopping power than the 9.65 mm (0.38 in), it entered service in 1911 and, in slightly modified form as the M1911A1, is still in production three-quarters of a century later, sure

tribute to a sound design. The Colt is a recoil-operated automatic of conventional design apart from the barrel stop mechanism which employs locking lugs and a swing link instead of the more usual receiver stop. It has both a grip safety (ie, cannot be fired unless it is firmly held in the hand) and a manual safety switch. The magazine holds seven rounds but an eighth can safely be left in the chamber. Barrel length is 128 mm (5 in) and this imparts a muzzle velocity of 252 m/sec (827ft/sec) to the heavy 14.95 g (230 gr) 0.45 in bullets; a man hit by such a slug stays down. However, because the gun itself is heavy (1.36 kg (3 lb)) and the recoil harsh, it is a difficult weapon to aim and fire accurately. (An unusual feature of the M1911 introduced during World War 2 as a survival tool for downed aircrew was a 'shotgun' cartridge firing tiny steel splinters. This was intended for fishing but it was found to be very effective against the enemy at close quarters!) The Colt was also manufactured in Spain by Star but was not so well made and tended to be unreliable, so was never as well favoured by German soldiers as 'the real thing'.

Once the Germans invaded the Soviet Union plentiful numbers of the Tokarev 7.62 mm Model TT 1930 and '33 fell into their hands and were widely used thereafter. This was virtually a copy of the Colt, using the same barrel locking system, but firing a much smaller bullet only 5.65 g (87 gr) in weight. The other main difference was that the Russians greatly simplified manufacture, enabling the weapon to be produced more quickly and cheaply than the American pistol. It has an 116 mm (4.57 in) barrel which imparts a muzzle velocity of 420 m/sec (1,378 ft/sec), giving an effective range of 50 m (55 yd).

Apart from the antiquated French designs mentioned above, by the time of the Second World War the only other modern armies to utilize revolvers as opposed to automatic pistols were those of Britain and the Empire countries. As a combat weapon a revolver is far less effective than an automatic, carrying a smaller number of rounds and having to be manually reloaded cartridge by cartridge rather than by the simple insertion of a fresh clip or magazine — an obvious disadvantage in the middle of a firefight. For these reasons, although British Webley and Anglo-American

Smith and Wesson revolvers were prized as souvenirs, they were not regarded highly by the German armed forces as weapons. The only real advantages revolvers have over automatics is that they are more robust, simpler to strip and clean and less prone to jamming. Inevitably a few must have been used on occasion by the Waffen-SS, but not in sufficient quantities to be significant.

Final mention must be made here of one unique type of military pistol which is known to have gone into limited production for purchase by German officers as a last ditch self-defence weapon. Four short 6.35 mm barrels were attached to a plate concealed behind a standard size rectangular belt buckle; pressing a catch caused the buckle plate to flip upwards revealing the barrels, which were fired by simple thumb action hammers. Such a weapon would not easily be detected in a cursory search and could obviously have presented a nasty surprise to a man's captors. An unexplained feature of this pistol is that the design of the eagle on the front of the buckle is neither Wehrmacht nor SS style. Only one example is known to survive.

Sub-machine-guns

A sub-machine-gun can be broadly regarded as a garden hose spraying bullets instead of water. It is generally of limited range and poor accuracy, and is effective through the sheer volume of fire poured out in a very short space of time. It is more compact and usually lighter than a rifle of equal calibre, and can be made very simply out of mainly stamped rather than machined components, reducing cost and increasing productivity at the same time. Germany was the main pioneer of this class of weapon and the Second World War MP 38/40, popularly though inaccurately known as the 'Schmeisser', has entered gun legend alongside the P 08 Luger, 'broomhandle' Mauser and a few others.

Hugo Schmeisser began work on a new, rapid-fire gun for infantry use in 1916 and his original design, designated MP 18, reached the troops in time for the last unsuccessful mass assaults on the Western Front in 1918. This had the same 32-round drum (or 'snail') magazine designed for the long-barrelled Luger variants, a rifle-style wooden stock and a perforated barrel sleeve to provide air cooling. In 1928 production was re-instated but the later weapon, designated MP 28, differed significantly in having a 20 or 32-round box magazine inserted into the receiver from the left-hand side, as well as single-fire capability in addition to fully-automatic. It was a very good weapon, more robust than the later cheap metal-stamped designs, but consequently heavier, more expensive and more laborious to manufacture. An irony is that this older but better-made weapon found its way into the hands of many Waffen-SS troops during the early part of the war because MP 38/40 production was principally destined for the Army! The SS recipients must have been delighted.

The MP 28 weighed 5.24 kg (11.5 lb) with 32-round magazine and used the same straight-forward blow-back principle as on so many auto-matic pistols. Of standard 9 mm calibre, it had a barrel length of 200 mm (7.9 in) which imparted a muzzle velocity of 365 m/sec (1,198 ft/sec). Cyclic rate of fire was 350-450 rpm (ie, 17.5 20-round magazines a minute or 14 32-round magazines — but this rate could not be sustained, of course). Like all sub-machine-guns, its effective range was only around 200 m (220 yd) and in combat it would normally not be used much above half this.

Although the MP 38 which appeared in 1938 shared a similar blow-back mechanism and 9 mm Parabellum ammunition, its design had nothing to do with Hugo Schmeisser and it was principally manufactured by Erma. However, some production was sub-contracted to Haenel, where Schmeisser worked as senior designer, and this is the most likely explanation for the weapon being popularly even if erroneously called the 'Schmeisser'. It was the first sub-machine-gun in the world to dispense with a wooden stock, having a folding tubular steel shoulder rest instead, but was otherwise of conven-tional machined construction. A flaw in the basic MP 38 was that, when cocked, it could easily be fired accidentally, and a number of casualties resulted, so a safety pin was introduced on an in-terim model designated MP 38/40. Finally came the MP 40, which was basically the same weapon but simplified to speed up production and make it cheaper, stamped and cast components replacing as many as possible of the earlier machined ones and extensive use being made of welding.

All models had the same 32-round magazine in-

The man on the left is also carrying an MP 28. The officer on the right is Hermann Fegelein (BA 73/96/22).

Small arms

Gebirgsjäger wearing snowshoes and equipped with an MG 42 and MP 40 (BA572/1733/27a).

serted from beneath the barrel instead of from the side (as on the MP 28), but in practice only 27 or 28 rounds were normally loaded so as to reduce tension on the spring and help prevent jamming.

The MP 38/40 was one of the finest combat weapons of the war despite — or perhaps because of — its simplicity, and British, American and Soviet troops would all eagerly abandon their own weapons when they secured an abandoned or captured example. In the Wehrmacht and Waffen-SS it was initially issued to platoon and section leaders, paratroops and AFV crews but rapidly became far more widespread.

The definitive MP 40, of which most were produced, weighed 4.7 kg (10.36 lb) loaded, 4.08 kg (9 lb) empty, overall length with and without the folding stock extended being 833 and 630 mm (32.8 and 24.8 in). The barrel itself was 251 mm (9.88 in) long and imparted a muzzle velocity of 365 m/sec (1,198 ft/sec), combat range being 100-200 m (110-220 yd). The MP 38 and '40 could be fired either with single, aimed shots or fully-automatically, the cyclic rate of fire being 500 rpm.

Even before the MP 38 came into service, the Bergmann company had produced an interim design which owed a great deal to the MP 28 and was similar in most respects except that the magazine loaded from the right-hand instead of the left-hand side. This was the MP 34/35 which remained in production in Germany and Denmark throughout the war and after 1940 was exclusively allocated to the Waffen-SS. Like the MP 28 it had a wooden stock and a high proportion of machined components but it only weighed a fraction more than the MP 40 at 4.73 kg (10.43 lb). It was also much more reliable because instead of a sliding bolt in the side, which exposed the gun's 'innards' to dirt and grime, it had a bolt at the rear. It also had a higher cyclic rate of fire of 650 rpm due to its superior manufacturing quality, but the ammunition fired, muzzle velocity and combat ranges were all otherwise identical, despite the fact that the barrel was shorter at 200 mm (7.87 in). The SS troops appreciated another aspect of the MP 28 and '34/35 which would not be readily appreciated by anyone other than a soldier; the sideways-mounted magazines enabled them to be fired from a prone position or from a trench or foxhole more easily and

Below left *A fully kitted-out Gebirgsjäger in pristine smock and white cap cover with snow goggles, skis, an ice axe and rope, binoculars and an MP 40 (BA 572/1732/8a).*

Right *Brutal-looking gang of thugs from the infamous Dirlewanger 'Division' during the Warsaw uprising in August 1944. Under a magnifying glass the crossed rifles and stick grenade collar patch insignia can be seen on the foreground MP 40-toting man* (Ullstein Bilderdienst via Chris Mason).

Below *The foreground SS grenadier in this picture has an MP 40 slung across his back (BA 81/144/9a).*

Inset *Trying out the Italian Beretta 9 mm Model 1938, designated MP 739(i) by the Germans. Although the user is an Army Gebirgsjäger, the picture is included because it shows the weapon so clearly* (BA 312/999/21a)

Main picture *The MP 739(i) in Fallschirmjäger hands* (BA585/1846/13a).

with less exposure than the MP 38/40 permitted, with its long downwards-pointing magazine.

Another SMG which was almost exclusively used by the Waffen-SS and military police was the 9 mm Steyr-Solothurn S1-100 machine pistol, an Austrian design designated MP 34(ö) in German service. It was similar in appearance to the MP 28, with a wooden stock, perforated barrel sleeve and 32-round box magazine inserted from the left, but had a fore sight as well as an adjustable rear sight and metal plate on the left of the forward part of the stock instead of a thumb groove in the wood, as well as the curvatures and definition of the stock being sharper. It fired the standard 9 mm Parabellum round, had a 200 mm (7.87 in) barrel like the MP 28 and '34/35, and a muzzle velocity of 418 m/sec (1,372 ft/sec); this extended its effective range in capable hands to some 300 m (330 yd). The 9 mm Czech ZK 383 was also similar in general appearance apart for the existence of a bipod attached to the centre of the barrel to stabilize it for the light machine-gun (LMG) role. The reason for this provision was that the gun had two rates of fire, 500 or 700 rpm, adjusted by adding or removing a small weight on the breech block. In addition, it had a far longer barrel, 325 mm (12.8 in) in length, which imparted a muzzle velocity of 365 m/sec (1,198 ft/sec) and allowed the weapon to be fired out to approximately 500 m (500 yd) with a fair measure of accuracy when its bipod was used.

Germany's Hungarian ally also produced a sub-machine-gun in 1943, the 9 mm Model 43, but I have only seen a drawing of this and no data is available. It was of unconventional design with a wooden forestock but folding metal rear stock and pistol grip. The 30-round magazine folded forwards and upwards into the forestock when the weapon was not in use. This SMG would have partially equipped the Hungarian 25th and 26th Waffen Grenadier Divisions der SS. Similarly, the Italians produced their own design, the 9 mm Beretta Model 38 which is considered by many people one of the finest such weapons of the War. The Germans appropriated large numbers after Italy's surrender in 1943 and kept it in production for their own troops in Italy and the Balkans. It is a very strongly constructed weapon with a full wooden stock, perforated barrel sleeve and a firing mechanism similar to that on the Steyr-Solothurn. The quality of its manufacture deteriorated as the War progressed as more stamped metal components were introduced and the ventilated jacket was abandoned, but it was superbly balanced and on single-shot could be aimed accurately at 300 m (330 yd). It could accept 10, 20, 30 or 40-round magazines of standard 9 mm Parabellum cartridges. Barrel length is 315 mm (12.4 in) and muzzle velocity 420 m/sec (1,378 ft/sec). Unusually, the Beretta has two triggers, one for single-shot and the other for automatic fire, cyclic rate in the latter mode being 400-500 rpm. The Rumanian Orita SMG was a simplified copy similar in appearance but with a shorter barrel (287 mm (11.3 in)) and lower muzzle velocity (390 m/sec (1,280 ft/sec)); it only had a single trigger.

The Finns who fought as the third battalion of the *Nordland* Regiment within the 5th SS Division *Wiking* contributed yet another SMG to the Waffen-SS, the Suomi M/1931 which had already proved itself a well-made and reliable weapon during the Winter War of 1940. It had a beautifully-crafted wooden stock and ventilated barrel sleeve, and all metal parts were machined, giving marvellous accuracy and reliability; jamming was virtually unknown. The quality of the craftsmanship made it a much-prized weapon since it apparently never wore out and never let you down. It employed a straightforward blow-back mechanism and was otherwise remarkable only in the fact that both box magazines containing 30 or 50 rounds, or a 71-round drum magazine could be fitted to the same weapon. The principal penalty for the latter feature was that weight went up to 7.04 kg (15.52 lb), making it virtually 50 per cent heavier than any other Second World War SMG. Barrel length of the 9 mm M/1931 is 314 mm (12.36 in) and muzzle velocity 400 m/sec (1,313 ft/sec), and like the Beretta it could be aimed and fired accurately out to 300 m (330 yd). Cyclic rate of fire with the drum magazine is 900 rpm.

Inevitably, as with pistols the Army and Waffen-SS extended their armouries by means of other commandeered weapons from vassal states and those captured from the enemy. The British Lanchester SMG was a direct copy of the Bergmann MP 28 mostly issued to naval personnel and Commandos; the Sten, mass-produced from the cheapest and simplest materials for speed and economy as well as ease of maintenance, was a poor weapon, though effective in the long term because of the sheer number made and issued not just to British and Empire forces but to Resistance movements in the occupied countries. It was not, however, a weapon coveted by anyone, even though in the desperate days towards the end of the War the Germans themselves manufactured a copy for use by Volksturm units; the only significant difference between the MP 3008, as it was called, and the Sten lay in the fact that the magazine was inserted from beneath the barrel instead of from the side. The Australians realized the limitations of the Sten and produced their own Austen SMG which copied features both from the latter and from the MP 40. In Europe it was mainly used only in Italy so opportunities for examples to fall into Waffen-SS hands must have been rare;in any case the MP 40 was superior so captured Austens would probably just have been preserved as souvenirs.

The French MAS Model 1938 SMG was not greatly used by the Germans except on garrison duties in France, although it was used by the Vichy French and some may have found their way to members of the 33rd Waffen Grenadier Division *Charlemagne*. However, it used a unique calibre of 7.65 mm which made it incompatible with the standard German types of ammunition, and it also carried a lighter punch than a 9 mm weapon. It was of advanced design, with the recoil spring fully recessed into the wooden shoulder stock; this made the weapon's overall length a mere 623 mm (24.53 in), barrel length being 224 mm (8.82 in). Muzzle velocity is 350 m/sec (1,149 ft/sec).

Captured Soviet sub-machine-guns were inevitably much more widely-used by all the German forces. Earliest of these was the 7.62 mm PPD M1934/38/40 which, in typical Soviet fashion, 'inherited' features from the two best Western European SMGs available for study at the time it was designed, the Finnish M/1931 and the German MP 28, both of which it closely resembled in general appearance. However, manufacturing standards were far lower in general, although the Russians pioneered one technique now often used in SMG construction, namely chrome-plating the barrel to reduce wear and facilitate cleaning. The PPD has a wooden stock, ventilated barrel sleeve

and can accommodate either a 25-round box or a 71-round drum magazine beneath the barrel, which is 269 mm (10.6 in) long. In German service it was found that all Russian small arms of 7.62 mm calibre would accept Mauser 7.63 mm rounds so ammunition was not a problem. The PPD has a muzzle velocity of 488 m/sec (1,602 ft/sec) and a cyclic rate of fire of 800 rpm but effective range is less than that of the Suomi and similar to the MP 28's at about 200 m (220 yd).

When the Germans invaded the Soviet Union many arms manufacturing plants were rapidly overrun, including those producing the PPD, and Russian industry was moved east. To replace the PPD the 7.62 mm PPSh 41 was then put into production, a simplified version of the same weapon but with the wooden stock cut off square in front of the magazine receiver. This, the use of cheap sheet steel stampings in the manufacture of components and a small reduction in barrel length to 265 mm (10.43 in) slightly reduced the gun's weight from 5.7 to 5.4 kg (12.5 to 11.9 lb). It was manufactured in untold millions and issued to all the men in assault regiments regardless of rank; consequently it was captured in such vast quantities that it became the second most common German SMG after the MP 38/40! German industry even bent to the task of converting the weapon to accept 9 mm cartridges to ease the supply demands on indigenous weapons. The PPSh could either accept the 71-round drum magazine or a new, enlarged, 35-round box type, maximum cyclic rates of fire being 700-900 rpm; muzzle velocity and range are the same as on the earlier PPD.

One of the most remarkable of all Soviet weapons was the 7.62 mm PPS 42, designed like the British Sten as an emergency weapon when the hour seemed darkest and the people of Leningrad were steeling themselves to their city's epic siege. It was designed by an engineer, A. I. Sudarev, and construction was farmed out to local light metal plants. It was made entirely of sheet metal parts welded, riveted, bolted or pinned together according to available resources and, as might be expected of such an improvised weapon, was crude and unsophisticated in appearance. But it worked, which was the main thing, and even after the siege was lifted remained in production with a few refinements as the PPS 43, being manufactured in

large quantities. It had a standard 35-round box magazine and could fire on fully automatic only, entirely lacking a single-shot capability. Barrel length is 254 mm (10 in), rate of fire 700 rpm and effective range 100-200 m (110-220 yd). (It should in passing be noted that all Soviet box magazines are curved or banana-shaped, rather than straight. The reason for this is simply that their standard Tokarev 7.62 mm cartridges are bottle-shaped so introducing a curvature to the magazine allows more rounds to be packed into a box of smaller vertical dimensions than would be possible with a straight magazine.)

Final mention must be made of the four American sub-machine-guns which the Germans inevitably started to capture — though never in large quantities — from 1943 onwards, particularly the famous Thompson M1928 which put the name 'Tommy-gun' into the English language. This, the M3 'Grease Gun' and the Reising M 50/55 were all of 0.45 in (10.43 mm) calibre, while the fourth and least known, the private-venture UD M'42, was a 9 mm weapon. The M1928 derived from a belt-fed light machine-gun designed during the First World War but which did not enter military service. During the 1920s it was constantly remodelled and became almost a symbol of Prohibition gangsterism, but it was not until 1928 that the American Army expressed an interest. By this time the Thompson was well developed. Being designed for commercial rather than military sale, it was precision engineered with a wooden butt, wooden pistol grip and wooden forestock which also had a pistol grip, both elegantly tooled with individual finger grips (these were simplified on the later military M1 model and on the final M1A1 the front grip under the barrel was abandoned entirely). Again, being designed for commercial sales rather than military mass-production, it was a complicated though robust design operating on the blow-back principle which could accept either a

Men of the Das Reich *Division during Operation 'Citadel' — the battle of Kursk. The soldier on the right holds a captured Soviet PPSh-41 sub-machine-gun* (BA 81/143/6a).

50-round drum magazine or 20 or 30-round box magazines; the drum could not be fitted to the M1/M1A1. Other simplifications on the military versions included deletion of the long-range back sight (calibrated to 550 m (602 yd)), of the cooling fins on the barrel (similar to those on a motor cycle cylinder block), and of the vents in the top of the front of the barrel which were designed to help prevent the weapon riding up when fired (a fault of all SMGs) by providing a certain amount of automatic down pressure.

The Thompson was a sophisticated and popular weapon and captured examples were highly prized by the Germans, despite the frequent difficulty of obtaining American 0.45 calibre ammunition. Essential characteristics of the M1 are a barrel length of 267 mm (10.5 in), muzzle velocity of 280 m/sec (920 ft/sec), cyclic rate of fire of 700 rpm and effective range of 200-300 m (220-330 yd), although under normal combat situations 100 m (110 yd) should be taken as the norm.

The M3 'Grease Gun' was the American Army's answer to the various cheap sub-machine-guns being mass-produced in Europe, although it was principally used in the Far East and, like the Sten, was not a greatly desirable weapon. Apart, inevitably, from the barrel and breech block and a couple of other minor components which had to be machine-finished, it was constructed of stamped and welded steel and had the same unfinished, unpolished appearance as the other weapons rushed into production as war emergency measures. Indeed, its very nickname indicates its close resemblance to the garage mechanic's tool. It was a very simple blow-back weapon with no refinements, firing fully-automatic only with no single-fire selector mechanism and not even a safety catch. Captured examples would probably have been thrown away by the Germans, if it were not for the fact that it had been deliberately designed to be easily convertible to 9 mm calibre as a weapon to equip Resistance forces, who would themselves mostly have access to captured German ammunition. With a barrel length of 203 mm (8 in) and a muzzle velocity of 280 m/sec (919 ft/sec) it was a highly inaccurate and short-ranged weapon — indeed, rarely used over 50 m (55 yd) — which is why it found more success during the close jungle and island fighting of the Far East than in the more open battlefields of Europe.

The two other American SMGs were oddities, the Reising Model 50/55 using a complex retarded blow-back mechanism which was prone to breakdown and having other features which allowed dirt to get into its moving parts rather too easily. It was a private venture, but the US Marine Corps took several thousand and others were exported to the Soviet Union. Being an inferior weapon to the Thompson yet still of the same large calibre which German ammunition would not fit, it was only used in tiny and insignificant quantities by the Axis powers. The same comment applies to the UD M'42, another private venture weapon though this time of standard 9 mm calibre, designed by Marlin (more famous for their shotguns). Most of the relatively small number supplied to the US armed forces found their way into the hands of the OSS (Office of Strategic Studies) and various Resistance organizations, so captured examples used by the Waffen-SS would have predominantly been within units entrusted with anti-Partisan duties, such as the *Prinz Eugen* Division.

Rifles and carbines

The rifle and the carbine, the latter originally designed for cavalry use, have been the standard infantry weapons for over a hundred years, so it was inevitable that by the time of the Second World War an enormous number of different types existed, many of them of quite elderly design. The Germans naturally acquired millions of rifles as they overran Europe and western Russia and large quantities were pressed into service, rechambered to accept standard German 7.92 mm rifle cartridges where necessary. Probably the most influential rifle of all time is the Mauser Gew 98 (Gew = *Gewehr* — rifle), an improved version of a weapon first produced in 1888 which remained in production with minor modifications throughout both World Wars. It was widely copied by many other countries.

The Gew 98 is a bolt action single-shot rifle with a 5-round magazine and three bolt-locking lugs for safety. The standard rimless, bottle-necked 7.92 mm rounds are 80 mm (3.15 in) long, the bullet weighing 12.87 g (408 gr), propellant charge being

3.05 g (47 gr), although a shorter version 57 mm (2.24 in) long was also produced for use in converted Hungarian M35s (see below). The cartridges are inserted in clips into the magazine from above, working the bolt bringing each new round into the chamber as the expended cartridge is ejected. Whole clips do not have to be inserted so in action a soldier can fire one or more rounds and 'top up' the magazine at will rather than having to wait for the magazine to be exhausted — which can be inconvenient! The Gew 98 has a barrel length of 740 mm (29.1 in); this was reduced in the Kar 98 (Kar = *Karabiner* — carbine), a cavalry weapon, to 457 mm (18 in), then back up to 600 mm (23.6 in) in the Kar 98a, b and k which formed the standard German infantry weapons during the Second World War, although examples of the earlier models were still retained.

An interesting sidelight on Mauser development is that, because the Reichswehr was limited by the Treaty of Versailles to 100,000 men, armament manufacture was closely scrutinized and each soldier was limited to only 60 rounds of ammunition for training purposes, the Germans developed special training rifles to get around these restrictions. The first was a 4.5 mm (0.177 in) air rifle, the second a 5.58 mm (0.22 in) sub-calibre rifle, but they were otherwise identical in appearance and bolt operation to the full-size Mauser. With Hitler's rise to power these were used for training members of the Hitler Youth who, when they later entered the Army or Waffen-SS, would find no surprises in handling or stripping the Kar 98.

The Kar 98a came out in 1904, the principal difference between it and the basic '98, other than the barrel length, being that the bolt was turned down against the stock instead of projecting horizontally outwards, which made firing easier. This feature was retained on the '98b, which had the carrying slings mounted on the left side of the weapon rather than underneath the stock, and on the '98k which went into production in 1935 and utilized beech rather than scarce walnut in its stock. Sighting is by means of an inverted V at the front of the barrel and an adjustable V at the rear usually calibrated from 100-2,000 m (110-2,200 yd). In action, normal effective range was some 800 m (880 yd), but fitted with a telescopic sight for use by

Above *Parade of the Leibstandarte* Adolf Hitler *for swearing in officer candidates. In the foreground are a tripod of Kar 98s, an MG34 on its sustained fire tripod and an 8.1 cm mortar* (Christropher Ailsby Historical Archives).

Below *A variety of small-arms is in evidence here, including an anti-tank rifle, two MG 34s (one with tripod being assembled) and a Czech ZB vz.30, and an MP 38 or 40* (Christopher Ailsby Historical Archives).

Marksmanship practice for a Gebirgsjäger showing the correct prone attitude to be adopted when wearing skis. The weapon appears to be a Kar 98k (BA 101/821/36).

snipers this was more than doubled.

The Gew 98 weighs 4.2 kg (9.26 lb), the Kar 98k 3.9 kg (8.6 lb) without bayonet, overall length being 1,255 mm (49.4 in) and 1,110 mm (43.7 in) respectively and muzzle velocity 870 or 755 m/sec (2,855 or 2,478 ft/sec). The Gew 98 and Kar 98a were both manufactured in Poland from 1925 to identical specifications.

The 457 mm (18 in) barrel was reinstated in the Czech-built version of the Kar 98 which went into production in 1933 and was adopted into the German Army and Waffen-SS as the M 33/40, being widely used by mountain troops in particular such as the 6th SS Gebirgs Division *Nord*, 7th Freiwilligen Gebirgs Division *Prinz Eugen*, 13th Waffen Gebirgs Division der SS *Handschar*, 21st Waffen Gebirgs Division der SS *Skanderberg* and 24th Waffen Gebirgs Division der SS *Karstjäger*. The shorter barrel made the weapon more easily carried while rock climbing or using skis. In

addition, a steel spike could be attached to the stock as a climbing aid. Czech sources give muzzle velocity as 810 m/sec (2,658 ft/sec) but others only 640 (2,100), although the latter figure could have become confused in translation with that of the original Kar 98.

The Hungarian M35 rifle is often thought of as a Mauser derivative because it was so widely used by German troops but was in fact a Mannlicher design of broadly similar appearance and with the same 600 mm (23.6 in) barrel. However, it fired an 8 mm rimmed cartridge 56 mm long so it was easy to convert it to take the short 7.92 × 57 mm round referred to above and large numbers were used by the Hungarian units in the Waffen-SS. Performance was only marginally inferior to that of

Latvian SS snipers run to position themselves: the telescopic sight is clearly visible on the Kar 98 carried by the foregound figure (BA 81/142/35).

the Kar 98k, muzzle velocity being approximately 25 m/sec (82 ft/sec) lower.

Captured French Lebel, Berthier and MAS, and Russian Mosin-Nagant bolt-action rifles, were only issued to second-line troops on garrison duties, but this was not true of the Tokarev SVT 40 gas-operated semi-automatic self-loading rifles (SLRs) which had a rate of fire of 25 rpm, considerably in excess of any bolt-action design. Many of these were captured along with plentiful stocks of Soviet 7.62 mm ammunition and used in preference to the Kar 98 while German industry concentrated upon producing an indigenous SLR.

The SVT 40 was a development of the earlier Simonov design of 1936 which first appeared as the SVT 38 in 1938. Although the gas-operated recoil/reloading system was satisfactory, the gun was rather lightly built and parts tended to break under sustained use, so it was re-engineered as the SVT 40 which was much more robust. The weapon had a vicious recoil so it was fitted with a small muzzle brake, although even this did not effect a great improvement. What was significant, though, was that here was a weapon with the range of a conventional rifle but the rapid fire effect (admittedly only in short bursts) of a sub-machine-gun. The Tokarev weighs 3.89 kg (8.58 lb), takes a 10-round magazine and has a barrel length of 625 mm (24.6 in) which gives a muzzle velocty of 830 m/sec (2,724 ft/sec). Maximum range is 1,500 m (1,640 yd).

Mauser had already done some work on self-loading rifles during the First World War, but the Army had discouraged further work along these lines, preferring to develop the light machine-gun instead. Encounters with the Tokarev rapidly showed their mistake and both Mauser and Walther embarked on a crash programme to produce a home-grown SLR. Both used a similar gas-operated system whereby the expanding gas created by firing a cartridge is trapped by a cone screwed on to the end of the barrel. Sufficient gas is pushed backwards through vents at the rear of the cone to push back a piston enclosed in a barrel sleeve. The piston in turn pushes a connecting rod which automatically brings a new cartridge into the chamber. This system produced rather heavy and clumsy weapons but the Walther model was adjudged marginally superior and went into limited production as the Gew 41(W).

The Gew 41 weighs 5.03 kg (11.09 lb) and has a barrel 546 mm (21.5 in) long. It has a wooden stock with the 10-round box magazine being inserted through this from the bottom, just in front of the trigger guard, ammunition being the standard German 7.92 mm round. The sights are graduated from 100-1,200 m (110-1,313 yd) but normal combat range is again around 800 m (880 yd). Muzzle velocity is 776 m/sec (2,547 ft/sec). However, the Gew 41 was not a success with the troops in the field and was subsequently modified as the Gew 43 using a tap in the barrel copied from that on the Tokarev to trap the expanding gas and operate the reloading mechanism. This resulted in a lighter and more reliable weapon which was immediately popular and produced in large quantities.

The Gew 43 weighs 4.4 kg (9.7 lb) and has a barrel 549 mm (21.6 in) in length. Early production versions had a wooden stock but later war stringencies increasingly dictated the use of plastic. It also has a 10-round magazine, barrel length and muzzle velocity being the same as on the Gew 41. Unusually, the locking handle is on the left-hand side of the breech. The foresight has a protective hood. It was also manufactured with a barrel 50 mm (1.97 in) shorter as the Kar 43, in which greater use was made of stamped and cast components to save time and expense, but performance was essentially the same under combat conditions. The Kar 43 could also be fitted with a telescopic sight for use by snipers.

A final weapon which must be mentioned because I have seen photos of Waffen-SS troops carrying it is the American Winchester M1/M2 carbine of 0.30 in (7.62 mm) calibre which was designated SKb 455(a) by the Germans (SKb = *Selbsladekarabiner* — self-loading carbine). Over six million M1s were manufactured during the war and thousands fell into German hands during 1944-45, their light weight being greatly appreciated. The Winchester was a gas-operated carbine with a 15 or 30-round box magazine; the M1 was single-shot only but the M2 which succeeded and supplemented it had a fully-automatic facility. Barrel length is 457 mm (18 in), muzzle velocity 600 m/sec (1,969 ft/sec) and combat range 300 m (330 yd). The weapon only weighs 2.36 kg (5.2 lb).

Assault rifles

In the modern world the assault rifle reigns supreme as the principal infantry arm of virtually every national army, terrorist group and counter-insurgency unit, but it was a concept which took a long time to be developed in Second World War Germany, and then only despite Hitler's express wishes! The combined experience of both World Wars showed clearly that the vast majority of infantry engagements took place at under 500 m (547 yd) range, yet the standard bolt action rifles, and even the later SLRs, were calibrated out to 1,000 m plus. Sub-machine-guns and machine pistols fulfilled the close range demand, so what was obviously needed was a weapon combining a rapid-fire capability with ordinary rifle accuracy in this critical mid-range zone, from approximately 250-750 m (273-820 yd). Such a weapon would also remove a great deal of the infantry's dependence on machine-guns, whether light or heavy, although a continuing need for the heavier sustained-fire automatic weapons has been well proven in many post-war conflicts.

Theorists argued, correctly, that a fully-automatic rifle capable of operating in this middle zone would not require such a large cartridge or propellant charge, so more rounds could be contained in a magazine of given size. Therefore in 1934 research began into the best way of utilizing such a short round, research which paid dividends in another way, too, because by 1940 it resulted in a short (German *kurz*) round ideal for the Hungarian M35 bolt action rifle mentioned earlier. However, Hitler was opposed to development of new weapons firing pistol-calibre ammunition so the principal designers, Walther and Haenel, disguised their projects under the name *Maschinenpistole* instead of *Maschinenkarabiner* and continued their studies regardless of *Der Führer's* wishes! The result was the MP 43 designed at Haenel by Hugo Schmeisser, which became one of the most influential weapons in the world as far as subsequent small-arms design is concerned and was immensely popular with the troops to whom it was issued — which included the premier Waffen-SS Panzer and Panzergrenadier divisions from the start. Apart from Haenel, the MP 43 was also manufactured by Sauer, Steyr and Walther. A year after it went into production its proven success was such that Hitler authorized a new and more accurate name for it, StG 44 (StG = *Sturmgewehr* — assault rifle).

The MP 43/StG 44 weighs 5.22 kg (11.5 lb) and is constructed of pressed and diecast components with a wooden or plastic shoulder stock. The 7.92 × 57 mm round contains a bullet weighing 7.8 g (120 gr), the propellant charge being 2 g (32 gr), and 30 are carried in the forward-curving box magazine below the breech. It is fired by similar means to the SLRs described above, a gas vent in the barrel driving a piston to actuate the chambering mechanism, but the weapon can be fired on full automatic as well as single-shot by pressing a selector button above the trigger. In the former mode, the weapon has a cyclic rate of fire of 800 rpm. Muzzle velocity from the 419 mm (16.5 in) barrel is 650 m/sec (2,133 ft/sec). In action the StG 44 proved robust and reliable and made each infantryman his own light machine-gunner. One strange accessory designed specifically for this weapon was a curved barrel adaptor and periscope sight attachment intended to allow it to fire around corners; if it had ever worked properly this would have been extremely useful in street fighting and for the crews of AFVs, but it did not and few such adaptors ever entered service.

A much simplified and more cheaply-made version of the StG 44 was introduced by Haenel in the closing months of the war. Designated *Volksturm Gewehr* (People's assault rifle), it was intended for use by the people's militia units formed from young boys and old men to help in the last-ditch defence of the Reich. It has a barrel of

An MP 43 assault rifle being carried by a German mountain trooper (BA 90/3938/36).

378 mm (14.9 in) and the same muzzle velocity as the StG 44 but can fire on single-shot only and has a limited effective range of some 300 m (330 yd).

Going back in time, though, at the same time as Haenel was working on the MKb 42 which became the MP 43, Rheinmetall were busy developing a lightweight assault rifle for the Luftwaffe's paratroops and field divisions. The result was one of the most remarkable weapons of the war, the FG 42 (FG = *Fallschirmjäger Gewehr* — Paratroop rifle) which inevitably found its way into the hands of Otto Skorzeny's two SS *Fallschirmjäger* battalions. It was a weapon of lightweight construction with some machined but mostly die-stamped parts. Gas-operated, it incorporates a

Left *One of the SS Fallschirmjägers who took part in the rescue of Mussolini from Gran Sasso poses with his FG 42 automatic rifle in front of one of the DFS 230 gliders used in the assault* (BA 567/1503A/1).

Above *The FG 42 in use* (BA 576/1831/27a).

mechanism whereby the bolt remains open when automatic fire is selected, helping keep the weapon cool. The FG 42 weighs only 4.53 kg (10 lb) and has a side-mounted box magazine containing 20 standard-length 7.92 mm rounds. With a barrel length of 502 mm (19.76 in), these have a muzzle velocity of 761 m/sec (2,498 ft/sec), cyclic rate of fire being 750-800 rpm. Maximum effective range is 1,200 m (1,313 yd) when used in the light machine-gun mode using the bipod legs which fold down from underneath the barrel.

The FG 42 was complex to manufacture and only some 7,000 were made in total but it was a greatly prized weapon and extremely effective, having considerable influence on post-war LMG design.

Infantry support weapons

Machine-guns

The German Army and the Waffen-SS had, without a shadow of doubt, the finest machine-guns of the war in the MG 34 and its successor, the MG 42 (MG = *Maschinengewehr* – machine-gun), and also used a variety of captured weapons as the war progressed. Under the terms of the Treaty of Versailles Germany was prohibited from developing or manufacturing machine-guns. However, the Reichswehr overcame this restriction by having the work done by Solothurn in Switzerland, although the actual designing was undertaken by Rheinmetall-Borsig. The first weapon to go into production as a result of this programme was the MG 15 for the Luftwaffe which had a 75-round double or 'saddle' type drum magazine, and this was followed by the 7.92 mm MG 34 general-purpose machine-gun. Of comparatively lightweight construction, this could be mounted on a bipod in the LMG role or a substantial tripod for sustained fire duties; in either case either the 'saddle' magazine or 50-round belts

Left *Enormous numbers of captured weapons fell into the hands of the Waffen-SS. These are obsolete First World War German 7.92 mm sMG 08 heavy machine-guns captured from the Poles in September 1939* (Fred Stephens).

Above *The same weapon being used for training purposes by SS troops pre-war* (via Fred Stephens).

could be fitted. The former was an ingenious contraption: the individual rounds were not linked but each drum either side of the barrel was spring-loaded and rounds were fed into the chamber from each side alternately. The belts consisted of individual rounds of long 7.92 mm cartridges held together by what were in effect little more than paper clips, which made clearing a jammed round very easy. The belts were carried in rectangular mild steel boxes.

Being a general-purpose weapon, the MG 34 had an air-cooled barrel ventilated by circular holes in the sleeve rather than the heavy and cumbersome water jacket used in conventional heavy machine-guns. Air-cooling is not, of course, as efficient as water-cooling, so barrels overheated quite rapidly and for this reason were designed so that they could be unlocked and replaced in a matter of seconds: each gun crew of two men carried at least two and sometimes as many as six spare barrels in containers on slings across their backs.

The MG 34 remained in production from 1934 until 1945 although it was later supplemented by the Mauser MG 42. The basic weapon with its

Left *Loading belt links for an MG 34. Note early-pattern SS field caps with offset peaks* (BA 73/95/18).

Below left *Group of grenadiers in Russia with Kar 98ks and an MG 34* (Christopher Ailsby Historical Archives).

Above right *MG 34 team in Russia. Note the tripod for the sustained fire role being carried by the man on the extreme left, and the method of carrying the bayonet on top of the entrenching tool by the man in the centre* (Christopher Ailsby Historical Archives).

Right *Das Reich grenadiers dive for cover as they come under fire. The tube across the back of the centre man is a spare barrel container for an MG 34 or 42* (BA 73/83/72).

Left *Well-muffled SS grenadiers in Russia. Note the saddle drum magazine on the MG 34* (Christopher Ailsby Historical Archives).

Above *SS grenadiers with an MG 34* (Christopher Ailsby Historical Archives).

attached bipod (the tripod mounting was carried separately) weighs 11.5 kg (25.36 lb). (Compare this with a First World War MG 08 which weighed 62 kg (136.7 lb) *without* its mounting!) It has a wooden shoulder stock, a pistol grip, blade fore sight and V-notch rear sight, while a telescopic sight can be fitted for long-range use when the gun is mounted on its tripod. A ring sight for anti-aircraft use can also be fitted. The basic sights are graduated from 200-2,000 m (220-2,188 yd) and

the telescope out to 3,500 m (3,829 yd). A periscopic sight was also made so that the weapon could be fired from a trench or dugout without exposing the gunner's head. Barrel length is 627 mm (24.685 in) and muzzle velocity 755 m/sec (2,478 ft/sec), while cyclic rate of fire is as high as 800-900 rpm — ideal for use against low-flying enemy aircraft. The MG 34 can also be fired single-shot. It is recoil operated by means of a barrel baffle.

The weapon was extremely well-made — one might almost say too well-made because demand always exceeded supply. As well as being issued as an infantry weapon throughout the German armed forces, it was also mounted in most armoured fighting vehicles with a heavier-duty barrel which did not need to be changed so frequently.

In 1940 Mauser, using their existing experience

SS Fallschirmjäger with an MG 42, Russian front, 29 December 1944 (BA 76/100/26)

with the MP38/40 sub-machine-gun, began work on a new general-purpose machine-gun constructed more simply and cheaply than the MG 34 from largely die stamped and cast components. The MG 42, as it was designated when it entered production, was described in an American wartime intelligence manual as 'the most remarkable gun of its type ever developed' and it was rightly feared by all who came up against it, its tremendous rate of fire of 1,550 rpm producing a sound like ripping calico which no-one who has heard it can ever forget (the MG 42 can only be fired in the fully-automatic mode, no single-shot selector being fitted). Like the MG 34, the '42 has an air-cooled quick-change barrel with fitted bipod. Despite a shorter barrel — 533 mm (21 in) — than the MG 34, muzzle velocity and effective range are the same. The barrel change on the MG 42 is even quicker than on the earlier weapon, being effected by means of a simple spring catch. Overall weapon

weight is also 11.5 kg (25.36 lb). Belts or saddle drum magazines can be fitted, and as with the MG 34, individual belts can be clipped together for sustained firing. Both the MG 34 and '42 feature a small muzzle flash suppressor on the end of the barrel, not so much to conceal their presence from the enemy as to prevent the gunner becoming unsighted through partial blindness.

The German armed forces also used substantial numbers of Czech 7.92 mm ZB.vz 30 light and ZB.vz 37 heavy machine-guns (the weapons which provided the inspiration for the British Bren Gun and Besa machine-gun respectively). Both are gas-operated weapons unlike the recoil-operation MG

Although they are wearing SS-pattern camouflage smocks, these two soldiers may well belong to the Luftwaffe's Hermann Göring *Division, but the photo is included because it shows the Czech ZB vz.30 light machine-gun to advantage (BA 48/111/37A).*

Weapons of the Waffen-SS

34 and '42. The ZB.vz 30 is fed by means of a top-mounted 20 or 30-round box magazine and cocked by means of a prominent handle on top of the barrel, forward of the breech. Ammunition is standard German long 7.92 mm cartridges. Being a pre-war design like the MG 34, it is extremely well-constructed of largely machined components which made it expensive but also extremely strong and reliable. It was a popular weapon and used in large numbers by the Waffen-SS during the early part of the war, particularly when they were still fighting the Army for supplies. Overall weight is 10.04 kg (22.1 lb), barrel length 672 mm (26.45 in), muzzle velocity 762 m/sec (2,500 ft/sec), cyclic rate of fire 500 rpm and effective range 2,000 m (2,188 yd). The gun has a wooden stock, pistol grip and integral bipod mount.

The ZB.vz 37 is a heavy air-cooled machine-gun on a substantial tripod mounting, overall weight being 19 kg (41.8 lb). The barrel length is 678 mm (26.7 in) and a choice of two different cyclic rates of fire can be selected, 500 or 700 rpm; the slower rate would normally be used against ground targets, the higher against aircraft. (An extremely high rate of fire as on the MG 42 is actually very wasteful of ammunition and wears out the barrel rapidly.) Muzzle velocity is 792 m/sec (2,600 ft/sec) and the weapon is sighted from 300 - 2,000 m (330 -2,118 yd). The weapon is fed by 100 or 200-round belts.

The Germans also used captured French Mitrailleur Modele 1924/29 and Mitrailleuse Modèle 1931 light machine-guns and British Vickers heavy machine-guns captured in 1940 but only for second-line troops on garrison duties, as their calibres were incompatible with German ammunition. More substantial quantities of Soviet light Degtyarev 7.62 mm DP and heavy Degtyarev 12.7 mm DShK 38 and Goryunov 7.62 mm SG 43 machine-guns were used after capture (together with plentiful stocks of ammunition) in Russia.

The DP is a simple but brilliant weapon of basic construction containing only six moving parts which first went into production in 1928. Weighing 11.9 kg (26.23 lb) loaded (9.12 kg/20.1 lb unloaded), it has a wooden stock, rifle or (from 1944) pistol grip, ventilated barrel sleeve, flash suppressor, integral bipod and top-mounted flat pan-type drum magazine holding 47 rounds. The barrel length is 604 mm (23.8 in) giving a muzzle velocity of 840 m/sec (2,756 ft/sec), cyclic rate of fire being 500-600 rpm. It is a fully-automatic gas-operated weapon with no single-shot facility, effective range being about 800 m (875 yd).

Degtyarev's heavy DShK 38 is a belt-fed weapon of almost identical calibre and capability to the famous American Browning 0.5 in heavy machine-gun. However, it is a much heavier and more clumsy weapon, being mounted on a wheeled carriage with splinter shield dating back to the First World War. The gun itself weighs 'only' 33.3 kg (73.4 lb), but the total weight is 155.3 kg (342.4 lb), making it rather unmanoeuvrable. It employs the same type of gas-operated mechanism as in the DP and has a cyclic rate of fire of 550-600 rpm, the sights being graduated out to 3,500 m (3,829 yd). Barrel length is 1,002 mm (39.45 in) and muzzle velocity 860 m/sec (2,822 ft/sec). The metal non-disintegrating belts each contained 50 rounds.

The Goryunov SG 43 is also a belt-fed weapon which was normally mounted on a wheeled carriage, with or without splinter shield, although a more modern tripod was also produced. The basic gun weighs 13.8 kg (30.42 lb), the wheeled carriage 26.9 kg (59.3 lb) with shield, 23.09 kg (50.9 lb) without, and the tripod 13.9 kg (30.6 lb). The belts were sensibly longer than on the DShK 38, each containing 250 7.62 mm rounds. Barrel length is 719 mm (28.3 in), muzzle velocity 863 m/sec (2,832 ft/sec) and rate of fire 250 rpm against ground targets, 600-700 rpm when employed in the light anti-aircraft role. Effective range is approximately 2,000 m (2,188 yd).

Mortars

The German armed forces employed three standard field mortars as well as making extensive use of captured weapons, especially Russian ones yet again. Mortars are by definition high elevation smooth-bore weapons firing fin-stabilized bombs on a high plunging trajectory. The firing tube is mounted on a baseplate and there is normally, though not universally, a bipod front support which can be adjusted to give different angles of elevation and therefore range. The bombs have a propellant charge in their bases ignited by the simple process of dropping them into the barrel to strike a firing pin at the bottom. Because they are rugged, cheap and extremely simple to

Walloon volunteers of the 5th SS Sturm Brigade in Stalingrad. Weapons are an MG 34 and a little 5 cm mortar (Christopher Ailsby Historical Archives).

Left and above right *Examples of the 8.1 cm sGrW 34 mortar in use, actually by Luftwaffe paras but included for their clarity of detail* (BA 549/740/22a and 577/1917/8).

manufacture, mortars are one of the most common of all infantry support weapons in all armies, but they are not classified as artillery, hence their inclusion in this chapter. This is an anomaly in military nomenclature, obviously, since a mortar is an indirect fire weapon relying as much upon observers and communications as a howitzer. Mortars are particularly valuable weapons in attacking entrenched positions, since their bombs drop almost vertically downwards, as well as in mountain warfare, but they are largely ineffectual except as area denial weapons in wide open spaces or during a fluid battle of manoeuvre. What they do achieve is giving the infantry a useful high explosive

capability beyond the range of hand or rifle grenades, even though until more recent years mortars were so inaccurate that one shot in ten on target was the average expectancy.

The three principal German mortars were the 5, 8 and 12 cm le GrW 36, m GrW 34 and s GrW 42 (*leichte, mittler* and *schwere* — or light, medium and heavy — *Granatewerfer*, or grenade-thrower), the suffix number indicating the year of introduction into service. The little 5 cm weapon was pathetically inadequate by Second World War standards. It only fired a 0.89 kg (1.96 lb) charge and range was a mere 500 m (547 yd), so by 1941 it had practically dropped out of use. The 8 cm (actually 8.1 cm) weapon was much more practical and remains a standard calibre in most armies to the present day. It fired a 3.4 kg (7.5 lb) bomb to a maximum distance of 2,400 m (2,626 yd). The 12 cm weapon, introduced after front-line experience of Soviet heavy mortars showed their value, fired a 15.79 kg (34.82 lb) bomb to a range of 6,050 m (6,619 yd). Extensive use was also made by the German armed forces of captured Soviet 82 and 160 mm mortars firing 3.35 and 41.1 kg (7.4 and 90.6 lb) bombs to maximum ranges of 3,100 and 5,150 m (3,391 and 5,634 yd) respectively. All varieties of mortar could be mounted in the SdKfz 250 and '251 armoured half-tracks (qv).

The 5 cm mortar was a company weapon capable of being fired at a rate of 23 rpm but blast radius of its projectile was a mere 9 m (9.85 yd). The 8.1 cm weapon was a battalion weapon and just as quick to reload but blast radius was almost double at 17 m (18.6 yd), while the latter factor was double again at 34 m (37.2 yd) for the 12 cm weapon issued at regimental level, although rate of fire was effectively halved.

Infantry anti-tank weapons, grenades and mines

At the beginning of the war Germany, like other nations, relied upon anti-tank rifles to give the infantry some protection against enemy tanks, but these rapidly proved ineffectual other than against light tanks and from 1942 various hollow-charge anti-tank weapons were developed.

Earliest of the German anti-tank rifles, excluding the 13 mm Mauser of 1918, was the PzB 38 (PzB = *Panzerbüchse* — literally, 'armour box' or 'tin', actually meaning anti-tank rifle). Designed by Rheinmetall-Borsig, this was chambered to accept a Mauser 13 mm cartridge into the crimped neck of which was inserted a solid 7.92 mm sub-calibre armour-piercing bullet. This system imparted a very high muzzle velocity of 1,210 m/sec (3,971 ft/sec) but the recoil was so fierce that the barrel, itself 1,090 mm (42.9 in) long, had to be designed to recoil within the stock. This recoil opens the breech and ejects the spent cartridge case. The weapon, which weighs 15.88 kg (35 lb), has a pistol grip, padded shoulder stock and a bipod mount.

In the interests of economy and more rapid production, a modified version appeared the following year, designated PzB 39. This was greatly simplified, a muzzle brake replacing the sliding barrel mechanism and the breech having to be opened manually after each shot. Overall weight was thereby reduced to 12.35 kg (27.23 lb) although barrel length remained the same and muzzle velocity was actually improved to 1,265 m/sec (4,152 ft/sec). The Solothurn 20 mm PzB 41 was also used in limited numbers, its late date into service meaning that it was completely ineffectual against Soviet T-34s and KV-1s. It was also a heavy and cumbersome weapon, overall weight being 44 kg (97 lb), but it was at least self-loading, speeding up the rate of fire. A 5 or 10-round box magazine fitted on to the breech on the left-hand side of the weapon, the mechanism being actuated by recoil. Barrel length of the PzB 41 is 910 mm (35.83 in) and muzzle velocity 735 m/sec (2,412 ft/sec).

With the discovery of hollow-charge, or high explosive anti-tank weapons which use a shaped explosive charge to blow a hole through the armour plating of a tank instead of relying on the kinetic energy in a high-velocity solid armour-piercing round, further development work on anti-tank rifles ceased completely and in 1942 the first German hollow-charge infantry weapon appeared. This was the Panzerfaust ('armoured fist', also known as the Faustpatrone — 'fist cartridge') developed by Dr Heinrich Langweiler at Hugo Schneider AG. It was a very simple device consisting of a hollow steel tube 360 mm (14.2 in) long, a hollow charge grenade being fitted in one end and an explosive charge in the centre providing a counter-blast at the rear so there was no recoil. However, it had to be held at arm's length to fire, which made it impossible to aim! Langweiler therefore modified the design by lengthening the launching tube so that it could be tucked under the arm. The counter-blast gases were then expanded harmlessly behind the firer (although friendly troops nearby had to exercise caution). A simple foresight was fitted, and the weapon was designated Faustpatrone 30, the latter figure denoting its maximum range in metres (33 yd). The overall weapon weighs 5.2 kg (11.25 lb) and its hollow-charge grenade was capable of penetrating up to 140 mm (5.5 in) of armour plate at 30°, quite sufficient to knock out a T-34 or KV-1.

Above left *Grenadier with a Kar 98 fitted with an adaptor for firing rifle grenades* (BA 78/20/2a).

Above right *Standard stick grenades in the belt of an SS grenadier* (Christopher Ailsby Historical Archives).

However, it took a brave man to wait until a tank was within 30 m before firing, and in 1943 a more powerful version designated Faustpatrone 60 was introduced which had a range of 60 m (65.6 yd), followed in 1944 by a further-improved weapon which used a double propellant charge to give greater sustained thrust. This was the Faustpatrone 100 which had a range of 100 m (109 yd). The grenades themselves were fin-stabilized in flight, the fins folding against the shaft when the bomb was inserted into the muzzle and springing out upon firing.

The Germans also developed several hollow-charge anti-tank rifle grenades which could be fired from standard 7.92 mm rifles (including the PzB 39, when it was reclassified GrB 39 (GrB = *Granatebüchse* — grenade rifle)). An adaptor was fitted to the rifle's barrel and blank cartridges used to provide the propellant charge. These included the Gewehr Panzergranate (rifle anti-tank grenade), the Gross Gewehr Panzergranate (Gross = heavy), and the Gross Panzergranate 46 and 61. The earlier grenades were ineffective as anti-tank weapons, being limited to some 50 m (55 yd) range and only being able to penetrate roughly 30 mm (1.2 in) of armour plate — which is still sufficient to damage the tracks or engine covers, for example, and thus disable a tank sufficiently to take it out of action for a while. The later two weapons had ranges of 145-200 m (160-220 yd), armour penetration being 90 and 126 mm (3.54 and 4.96 in) respectively.

The Germans also had a hand-thrown anti-tank grenade, the Panzerwurfmine (L), an ingenious contraption with a hollow-charge warhead and a wooden throwing handle around which were four canvas fins which opened out in flight so the grenade impacted warhead-first. It could be thrown to a range of 30-40 m (33-44 yd) and could penetrate some 64 mm (2.5 in) of armour plate. It was similar in design to the famous German high-explosive fragmentation-type anti-personnel Stielgranate, or 'stick grenade', which could be thrown to a similar range — perhaps a little further in the hands of an athlete. This had a 0.62 kg (1.37 lb) charge with an effective blast radius of around 16 m (17.5 yd), making it far superior to the little Eiergranate or 'egg grenade' which only contained 0.34 kg (0.75 lb) of explosive and had a blast radius

of 13 m (14.2 yd), although in its favour the latter — weighing only 0.34 kg (12 oz) instead of 0.62 kg (22 oz) — could be thrown 20-25 per cent further.

Alongside these short-range weapons the Germans also developed one of the best infantry anti-tank weapons of the war, the RPzB 54 (RPzB = *Racketenpanzerbuchse* — rocket anti-tank gun) which was based upon the American bazooka, some of which fell into German hands following the Allied landings in French North Africa in November 1942 (Operation 'Torch'). Also known as the Panzerschreck ('tank terror') or more colloquially by the troops who used it as the Ofenrohr ('stovepipe'), it was a metal tube firing a rocket-propelled hollow-charge weapon of 8.8 cm calibre, ignition being by means of an electric trigger powered by a small dynamo as in a modern gas stove igniter rather than by a battery. It has a very basic shoulder stock and pistol grip, construction throughout being of the lightest and simplest materials. A small shield incorporating a

Left *Infantry with a RPzB 54. The gunner is wearing his gasmask to protect his face from the rocket's backwash* (BA 279/942/24).

Right *The 8.8 cm RPzB 54 'bazooka', here being demonstrated by a Fallschirmjäger team* (BA 578/1936/13a).

Weapons of the Waffen-SS

transparent plate for sighting was incorporated to protect the user's face from the rocket's backblast, but even so a gasmask was often worn to give extra protection from the fierce heat.

The RPzB 54 fires a circular-fin-stabilized projectile weighing 3.28 kg (7.23 lb) at a muzzle velocity of 105 m/sec (346 ft/sec); it should be remembered that muzzle velocity neither enhances nor detracts from the effectiveness of a hollow-charge weapon so is really irrelevant. The weapon itself minus bomb weighs 9.18 kg (20.3 lb). Effective range is approximately 100 m (109 yd) and armour penetration 100 mm (3.94 in). It was and is more accurate than any of the even simpler Panzerfaust models and had the great advantage of being able to be fired from a prone rather than a kneeling or standing position.

Mines are principally a defensive weapon designed to slow up an enemy advance or channel his forces into a 'killing ground' of one's own choice. Although there are many more types today, during the Second World War they were either of the fragmentation type designed for anti-personnel use or of the high explosive (and later shaped charge) variety designed as tankbusters. Mines are usually, though not universally, circular and fairly flat, depending upon a strong baseplate to deflect their blast upwards. They can either be detonated by pressure on a spring-laden fuze in their tops (the most common practice), by a trigger activated by the operator pulling on a wire attached to the mine's side when a suitable target passes over the weapon, or more recently by a radio impulse. Anti-personnel mines can also be of the 'jumping jack' variety pioneered by the Germans: a simple metal spike or tripwire activates a propellant charge in the base of the mine which throws it above the ground to explode at roughly waist height. These are the most difficult of all to detect because they are small and have a low metallic content.

The Germans utilized over 40 different types of mine of their own devising during the war, plus

SS infantry with a mine detector (Christopher Ailsby Historical Archives).

countless thousands lifted from Allied minefields during their various campaigns, so only the most common will be considered. One of the most abhorred by Allied troops was the S or Schützenmine which was produced in several variants with zinc, steel, glass, wood or concrete cases and fired a shrapnel charge vertically upwards at great hazard to a soldier's most precious possessions. Weighing roughly 0.5 - 4 kg (1-9 lb) in different variants and detonated by anything from as little as 2.7 kg (6 lb) to as much as 15.9 kg (35 lb)

ground pressure, these anti-personnel mines had blast radii of anything from 7-30 m (7.7-33 yd).

The most famous, or infamous, German mines of the war were the Tellermine anti-tank weapons, which existed in five basic variants. The earliest and lightest was the TMi 29, a light anti-tank weapon containing a 4.5 kg (10 lb) TNT charge capable of penetrating 20 mm (0.79 in) of armour plate — more than the lower hull plates of most wartime tanks. It was set off by a ground pressure of 91 kg (200 lb). Next came the TMi 35 which had a 9.5 kg

(21 lb) charge and was capable of penetrating some 30 mm (1.18 in) of armour plate; ground pressure to activate this weapon was 136 kg (300 lb). Finally, the TMi 35S, '42 and '43 had identical explosive charges of 5.44 kg (12 lb), armour-piercing ability of 24 mm (0.95 in) and were set off by a ground pressure of 147 kg (325 lb). The minor differences in their design were purely efforts to reduce their susceptibility to being set off by blast from nearby shell explosions.

The Holzmine ('wood mine') was a simple wooden box anti-tank weapon which could not be detected by magnetic sweeping devices. It contained 4.5 kg (10 lb) of high explosive and was detonated by a ground pressure of 90 kg (200 lb). It was copied by the Russians who also introduced an anti-personnel variant.

Two final types of German mine deserve special mention, the Haft-Hohlladung 3 kg hand-held magnetic anti-tank mine and the Riegel Mine 43, forerunner of the modern Bar Mine. The former was a conical shaped-charge device fitted with a carrying handle at the apex into which was fitted a detonator with a 4.5 second delay. The base was of plywood to which were bolted three horseshoe magnets. The device was used by tank killer squads who would leap from ambush to slap the mine against any reasonably flat portion of the vehicle's hull or turret. It was capable of penetrating 110 mm (4.33 in) of armour and thus destroying or disabling any known AFV. The Riegel bar mine was introduced in 1943, the basic idea being that a longer weapon was more likely to be driven over by an enemy vehicle than a smaller, circular device. Obviously, in a rectangular box mine it was impossible to employ any form of shaped charge, but the 4 kg (8.8 lb) charge was fully capable of blowing the tracks off any tank. It was a variable pressure-operated device detonated by 200 kg (440 lb) at either end or 400 kg (880 lb) in the centre.

The Germans also pioneered the use of what are today known as 'off-road mines'. A Panzerfaust could be tied to a tree, fence, corner of a building or any other suitable structure, with a cord putting tension on the trigger. This cord was extended across the adjacent road or track and when an unwary enemy vehicle drove over it the Panzerfaust was ignited, firing straight into its side from almost point-blank range. Many other similar improvized weapons were used, especially as the war dragged towards a close.

Flamethrowers

Next to napalm bombs, flamethrowers are the most terror-inspiring weapons known to man, the mere threat of their use frequently causing troops who would have endured artillery shells and machine-gun fire to surrender. The basic concept is a German one and flamethrowers were first used in significant numbers in 1915. There is an apocryphal story that the idea originated during a pre-war exercise when water hoses were used to soak the 'attackers'. The Kaiser, who was present at the time, asked the garrison commander what the idea was, and the quick-thinking officer replied that in time of war he would have been spraying petrol. Whatever the truth of this, the Germans had the first operational flamethrowers in use by 1914. During the Second World War, surprisingly, the Germans made less use of this type of weapon after the Polish and French campaigns than might have been expected, primarily because they are close-range devices designed for attacking strongpoints and of little value in an open battle of manoeuvre.

Any flamethrower consists basically of a tank of inflammable liquid, a cylinder of compressed gas, a valve and a nozzle tube with igniter. The main German weapons were the models 35, 40, 41 and 42 which only differed in weight, becoming progressively lighter as time passed from 35.8 kg (79 lb) to 18.4 kg (40.5 lb). All had a range of approximately 25 m (27-30 yd) and their tank capacity enabled them to fire ten one-second bursts. A throw-away weapon, the Einstoss-flammenwerfer 46 (single-shot flamethrower 46), entered service in 1944 and was issued to some Waffen-SS units as a last-ditch close defence weapon like some of the others already mentioned. As it name implies, it was a self-contained tube with fuel and propellant for a single burst, after which it was discarded.

An SS 10.5 cm leFH 18 beneath what seems a very inadequate camouflage net. Note field radio with extended aerial on left (Christopher Ailsby Historical Archives).

Weapons of the Waffen-SS

3. Artillery

When the title 'Waffen-SS' was formally adopted on 2 March 1940 its constituent components were the single regiment of the Leibstandarte *Adolf Hitler*, the SS Verfügungsdivision, SS *Totenkopf* Division and SS *Polizei* Division. By this time both the Verfügungsdivision, and the Leibstandarte were fully motorized, but deficient in artillery, while the *Totenkopf* Division, which had had to fight the hardest for military recognition by the Army authorities, still lacked much of the other equipment it needed. Then on, 23 March, Hitler intervened, overruling the high command and authorizing the formation of four heavy artillery battalions, one with 10.5 cm weapons for the Leibstandarte and one 15 cm unit for each of the three divisions. The *Polizei* Division, which was not considered a first line unit like the others, was only to receive older horse-drawn equipment. (It must be remembered that in 1940 the greater part of the German Army was still unmotorized. Only the ten Panzer divisions, seven Army infantry divisions and the elite *Grossdeutschland* Regiment shared the distinction of being fully motorized.)

The Leibstandarte received its artillery and tractors promptly, the Verfügungsdivision more slowly but still in time for the campaign in the west in May; the *Totenkopf* and *Polizei* formations had to make do with Czech equipment although, as George Stein has noted, this was not inferior to comparable German weaponry since Czechoslovakia had for years possessed one of the greatest armaments industries in Europe. In fact, as I remarked in *Hitler's Samurai* (Patrick Stephens Ltd), when General Max Weichs

inspected the *Totenkopf* for the first time on 4 April 1940 he was very surprised to find that instead of the poorly equipped foot division he had expected, Theodor Eicke's unit was in every way a modern, motorized formation.

Artillery is broadly divided into the following main categories: infantry guns, normally of 7.5 to 10.5 cm in calibre, issued at regimental level and above; field artillery of 10.5 to 15 cm calibre issued at divisional level; and heavy artillery of over 15 cm calibre issued at Corps level. However, these distinctions are far from absolute. For example, the German 7.5 cm leFK 18 (leFK = *leichte Feld Kanone* — light field gun) was classed as field artillery, the 15 cm sIG 33 (sIG = *schwere Infanterie Geschütz* — heavy infantry gun) was classed as an infantry weapon and the 10.5 cm sK 18/40 (sK = *schwere Kanone* — heavy gun) was classed as heavy artillery! These classifications apart, there is also anti-tank and anti-aircraft artillery and mountain and recoilless guns. (In the Waffen-SS, mountain guns were issued to the 6th SS Gebirgs Division *Nord*, 7th SS Freiwilligen Division *Prinz Eugen*, 13th Waffen Gebirgs Division der SS *Handschar*, the 21st Waffen Gebirgs Division der SS *Skanderberg*, and the 24th Waffen Gebirgs Division der SS *Karstjäger*, while Otto Skorzeny's two SS Fallschirmjäger battalions, Nos 500 and 600, had a number of recoilless weapons. The final category is rocket artillery. Heavy siege and coastal guns are excluded here because they were exclusively manned by Army and Navy personnel.

In the German Army and Waffen-SS, as the war progressed large numbers of artillery pieces were mounted on tracked or semi-tracked chassis to become self-propelled guns (SPGs) and these are described in this chapter. However, tank, assault gun and tank destroyer armament, except where a simple modification of a field or anti-tank gun sharing the same characteristics, is covered in the chapter on tanks and armoured fighting vehicles.

Infantry, field and heavy artillery

During the 1920s and '30s there was considerable debate within the German Army as to the relative merits of 7.5 cm as opposed to 10.5 cm weapons for the divisional artillery, with the larger calibre generally finding most favour. However, the 7.5 cm infantry guns then in existence, the IG 18 of 1927 and the IG L/13 of 1934 (IG = *Infanterie Geschütz* — infantry gun), were retained in service and in fact in 1944 two new designs were introduced, the IG 37 and IG 42. The IG 18 weighed 400 kg (882 lb) and fired a 6 kg (13.2 lb) shell with a muzzle velocity of 690 m/sec (2,264 ft/sec) to a maximum range of 3,375 m (3,692 yd). The IG L/13 weighed 376 kg (829 lb) and fired a 6.3 kg (13.9 lb) shell with a muzzle velocity of 225 m/sec (738 ft/sec) to a range of 3,840 m (4,200 yd). The later IG 37 and '42 both fired a 5.5 kg (12 lb) projectile with a muzzle velocity of 280 m/sec (919 ft/sec). The former had a lighter carriage, weight in action being 510 kg (1,124.5 lb) compared to 590 kg (1,301 lb) and also had greater elevation, 40° instead of 32°. Maximum range of the IG 37 was 5,150 m (5,634 yd), that of the IG 42 4,600 m (5,032 yd). An interesting hybrid weapon which also appeared in 1944 was the 7.5 cm FK 7M85. This was a combination of the barrel of the Pak 40 anti-tank gun on the carriage of the 10.5 cm leFH 18/40 (leFH = *leichte Feld Haubitze* — light field howitzer), and was an inspired attempt to give the 7.5 cm weapon greater elevation (42° compared with 22°) so that it could be used in the indirect fire role, and thus modified the gun had a range, firing a 5.4 kg (11.9 lb) shell, of 10,275 m (11,235 yd). (Later it was found that a relatively simple modification to the elevation mechanism of the basic Pak 40 could achieve the same result! This gun was known as the 7.5 cm FK 7M59, but only a very few were produced because it came too late in the War.)

While these 7.5 cm weapons were largely allocated to infantry formations at regimental level, there was also in existence from 1938 the leFK 18 (leFK =

leichte Feld Kanone – light field cannon) which was issued at divisional level until generally supplanted by 10.5 cm weapons. Even then, because of the need for lighter and more manoeuvrable guns that the larger calibre weapons, it was kept in production and improved as the leFK 38 which appeared in 1942 – something of a watershed year in German artillery development as will also be seen later. The leFK 18 weighed 1,120 kg (2,470 lb) and fired a 5.8 kg (12.79 lb) shell at a muzzle velocity of 485 m/sec (1,592 ft/sec) to a range of 9,425 m (10,311 yd); the leFK 38, which weighed 1,365 kg (3,010 lb) in action, fired a shell of the same weight but with a muzzle velocity of 605 m/sec (1,986 ft/sec) to give a range of 11,500 m (12,581 yd).

In reading these notes it should be remembered that in terms of German ordnance a *Geschütz* (gun) was usually a weapon with a fairly short barrel which nevertheless had a relatively flat trajectory, while a *Kanone* would normally be a weapon of the same calibre but with a longer barrel. A *Haubitze*, or howitzer, as in all armies was a weapon with a comparatively short barrel designed for firing on high trajectories.

First of the 10.5 cm guns to enter service was the leFH 18 in 1935 although it had been designed by Rheinmetall during 1928-29. Weighing 1,985 kg (4,377 lb), it fired a 14.8 kg (32.6 lb) shell with a muzzle velocity of 470 m/sec (1,542 ft/sec) to a maximum range of 10,675 m (11,675 yd). Over 5,000 examples were in service with the German armed forces by September 1939. However, it was soon felt that this gun's range was insufficient so from 1940 a muzzle brake was fitted to absorb the recoil of a more powerful propellant charge, and the resulting weapon, designated leFH 18M (M = *Mundungs-bremse* — muzzle brake), had a range of 12,325 m (13,480 yd). Some leFH 18s which had been sold to Holland in 1939 with this modification were captured in 1940 and taken into service as the leFH 18/39.

As the war progressed the infantry began to

Above right *Although the crew in this instance is actually Army personnel, this is a clear shot of the 10.5 cm leFH 18 in action* (BA 31/2415/16).

Right *An SdKfz 11 half-track towing a 10.5 cm leFH 18 field howitzer* (BA 208/19/11).

grumble increasingly about the weight of the leFH 18 so in order to lessen this in 1942-43 a number of 10.5 cm barrels were mounted on the carriage of the Pak 40 to produce the leFH 18/40. (This was at the same time that Pak 40 barrels were being mounted on leFH 18 carriages, possibly a unique situation in ordnance history!) This reduced the weight in action by 30 kg (66 lb), which was some help though not as much as the gunners would have liked. (The conversion did reduce the overall height of the gun, though, which was tactically beneficial especially when it was used in the direct fire role.) Meanwhile a new gun was also being designed which would be lighter and have a greater range. Krupp and Skoda both produced prototypes but the former, designated leFH 42, was not considered acceptable because, although its weight was only 1,630 kg (3,594 lb), it did not have any significantly greater range than the leFH 18M, so only the Skoda weapon went into production, entering service in 1944. Called the leFH 43, it was actually heavier than the leFH 18 at 2,200 kg (4,851 lb) but fired a heavier 14.8 kg (32.6 lb) round at 610 m/sec (2,002 ft/sec) to a range of 15,000 m (16,410 yd).

The leFH 43 was a revolutionary design at the time, and has been widely copied subsequently (particularly on the Soviet 122 mm D-30 field gun/howitzer which entered production in 1963 and is still current equipment). Instead of the standard split trail carriage, it had four outriggers, two in the normal position for trails and two which folded up underneath the barrel when the gun was being towed. When required for action, the forward pair of outriggers was lowered, the same mechanism simultaneously lifting the wheels off the ground to a position flanking the barrel. This ingenious arrangement not only lowered the weapon's height but also allowed it to traverse on its outrigger 'stand' through a full 360° — a most important and sometimes decisive ability in a fluid battle without a formal 'front line', such as characterized many encounters in Russia in particular. Hydraulic compensators further allowed each outrigger to be adjusted so that the gun would be horizontal on uneven or sloping ground.

Moving up to the 15 cm class, the first weapon to be considered is the sIG 33, classified as an infantry gun despite its calibre and weight of 1,700 kg (3,750 lb). Two were issued to each infantry regiment as the heavy artillery platoon, normally horse-drawn but towed by trucks or half-tracks in the motorized formations. First entering service in 1933, the gun fired a 38 kg (83.8 lb) shell at a muzzle velocity of 240 m/sec (788 ft/sec) to a range of 4,700 m (5,140 yd).

At divisional and Corps level the sIG 33 was com-

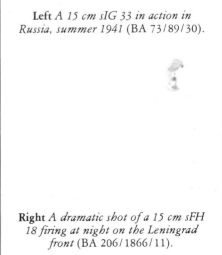

Left A 15 cm sIG 33 in action in Russia, summer 1941 (BA 73/89/30).

Right A dramatic shot of a 15 cm sFH 18 firing at night on the Leningrad front (BA 206/1866/11).

plemented by a number of other 15 cm guns and howitzers. (The 10 cm K18 of 1934 was too heavy for field use and was largely withdrawn for coastal defence duties by 1941, and its successor, the 10.5 cm sK 18/40 was little better and only produced in small quantities; so far as I know neither of these weapons was issued to Waffen-SS formations.) First of the post-First World War weapons to appear in the 15 cm class was the sFH 18 of 1934 which remained the principal heavy field howitzer throughout the war despite subsequent developments. Of conventional design with split-trail carriage, it weighed 5,512 kg (12,154 lb) in action and fired a 43.5 kg (95.9 lb) projectile. No fewer than eight different weights of propellant charges were provided, their use determined by range to target, but the largest of these, which gave a muzzle velocity of 495 m/sec (1,625 ft/sec) — high for a howitzer — was only used under exceptional circumstances because of the undue barrel wear it caused. Maximum range of the sFH 18 was 13,250 m (14,490 yd or 8.2 miles). Only a year after the sFH 18 went into production, the Army asked whether anything could be done to lighten it, as it was a very heavy load for the horse teams. Rheinmetall came up with a revised design incorporating aluminium alloy wherever possible in its carriage and recoil mechanism. To reduce stresses the barrel was shortened from 27 to 16 calibres* and a

muzzle brake was added. Entering production in 1938 as the sFH 36, it weighed 3,280 kg (7,232 lb), over two tonnes less than the sFH 18. As the war progressed, however, aluminium was increasingly needed for the aircraft industry and production ceased in 1942. The sFH 36 fired the same shell as the sFH 18 but muzzle velocity was lower at 485 m/sec (1,590 ft/sec) and range only 12,300 m (13,450 yd or 7.6 miles).

Two other 15 cm howitzers were designed during the war but never entered service, one a Krupp design which would accept bagged charges as brass for cartridge cases became scarce, and a Skoda design which was essentially a scaled-up 10.5 cm leFH 43. There was also a 21 cm howitzer, actually designated a long-barrelled mortar (*Lange 21 cm Mörser*), but this was unpopular and only saw limited service.

Complementing the howitzers were the heavy field guns, the 15 cm K 18 of 1938 and longer-barrelled K 39 of 1940 (only eight of which were produced), and the 17 cm K 18 of 1941. The 15 cm K 18 was an

* Length of barrel is always measured in 'calibres'. Thus the overall barrel length of the sFH 18 (405 cm (13.3 ft)) was 15 cm x 27, that of the sFH 36 15 cm x 16 = 240 cm (7.9 ft). In German service this length is denoted by the suffix L/ and the number of calibres (eg, L/24, L/71, etc). Generally speaking, the longer the barrel, the greater the muzzle velocity — which was particularly important in anti-tank guns — and range.

Above *A 15 cm sFH 18 with SS detachment* (BA 73/95/8).

Below *A wide angle lens gives a different view of a sFH 18 being manhandled with difficulty in the snow* (BA 101/837/30).

Below right *15 cm sIG 33 auf PzKpfw I* (BA 215/398/21a).

excellent weapon, weighing 12,760 kg (28,136 lb or 9.9 tons), which fired a 43 kg (95 lb) shell at a muzzle velocity of 890 m/sec (2,921 ft/sec) to a range of 24,500 m (26,800 yd or 15.2 miles). The 17 cm K 18 weighed 17,520 kg (38,632 lb or 17.24 tons) and fired a 62.8 kg (138.5 lb) shell with a muzzle velocity of 925 m/sec (3,036 ft/sec) to a range of 29,600 m (32,382 yd or 18.4 miles). Because of its weight it had to be transported in two loads and then laboriously assembled in the field.

The first self-propelled artillery piece to be possessed by the German armed forces was an improvisation, but it paved the way for a wide range of superior equipments. This was the sIG 33, a 15 cm sIG 33 infantry gun bolted (complete with wheels!) to a PzKpfw 1 tank chassis, which first appeared in 1939. Only 38 were built, by Alkett, but they gave slightly greater mobility to the motorized artillery regiments. Those which survived the French campaign went out to Africa with Rommel so were not therefore used by the Waffen-SS. In 1941-42 the same gun was mounted on the PzKpfw II chassis but very few were produced (exact number unknown) and it was of little significance. The same applies to the few sIG 33s mounted on PzKpfw 38(t) chassis.

Much more significant was the Wespe ('Wasp'), a 10.5 cm leFH 18M mounted in a lightly armoured open-topped superstructure on a PzKpfw II chassis. This Famo design stayed in production from 1942 to 1944, approximately 680 being manufactured, and it was widely used throughout the Army and Waffen-SS Panzer and Panzergrenadier divisions. The whole vehicle weighed 11.8 tonnes (11.6 tons). It was powered by a 6,191 cc Maybach HL 62 TRM six-cylinder water-cooled petrol engine which developed 140 bhp at 2,600 rpm, giving a top speed of 40 km/h (25 mph). Fuel capacity was 170 l (37.4 gal) which gave a road range of 140 km (87 miles), 90 km (56 miles) cross-country, and 32 rounds of ammunition were carried. Overall dimensions of the Wespe were length 4.81 m (15.8 ft), width 2.28 m (7.5 ft), and height 2.32 m (7.6 ft), and armour protection ranged from 14.5 to 20 mm (0.57 to 0.79 in). The same leFH 18M was also mounted on various French tank and tractor chassis, but these were principally used by second-line formations and for training. Eight were experimentally fitted to PzKpfw IV chassis by Krupp in 1942 but then attention switched to the 15 cm sFH 18.

From 1942 to 1944 Alkett and Deutsche Eisen-

A pair of Hummels in a desolate Russian landscape (BA 278/893/3).

werke produced 666 conversions of the PzKpfw III/IV chassis mounting this weapon in a similar open-topped superstructure to that on the Wespe. The Hummel ('Bumble Bee'), as it was known, was just as popular as the Wespe with the artillery regiments in the Panzer and Panzergrenadier divisions. It was a 23.5 tonne (23.1 ton) vehicle powered by a 11,867 cc Maybach HL 120 TRM V12 water-cooled petrol engine which developed 300 bhp at 3,000 rpm to give a maximum speed of 40 km/h (25 mph). Fuel capacity was 600 l (132 gal), giving a road range of 250 km (155 miles), 160 km (100 miles) cross-country, and 18 rounds of ammunition were carried. Overall dimensions of the Hummel were length 6.2 m (20.3 ft), width 2.95 m (9.7 ft), and height 2.85 m (9.4 ft), and armour ranged from 50 mm (1.97 in) on the hull front and 20 mm (0.79 in) on hull sides and rear to 14.5 mm (0.57 in) on the superstructure. The Hummel was a very effective weapon, used by all seven Waffen-SS Panzer divisions. (A virtually identical vehicle mounting the 8.8 cm Pak L/71 called Hornisse or

Nashorn is covered in the chapter on tanks and armoured fighting vehicles, as are other SP assult guns and tank destroyers.)

There were other experimental SP artillery pieces designed towards the end of the War but none reached the troops.

Anti-tank guns

One of the items the German Army and Waffen-SS most lacked at the outbreak of the Second World War was an effective anti-tank gun; by the end of the War German anti-tank technology was in the forefront of the world and their designs provided much of the groundwork for the weapons which equip today's most advanced tanks, including the British Challenger and the American M1 Abrams.

The first gun to enter service was the 3.7 cm Pak 35/36 (Pak = *Panzer Abwehr Kanone* — anti-tank gun) in 1933. It was first used by the Condor

Legion during the Spanish Civil War in 1936 and stayed in production until 1941, by which time over 20,000 had been manufactured, but its ineffectiveness had been noted during the campaign in the west in May/June 1940 and urgent demands for a replacement had been issued. It was a small and light gun, weighing only 432 kg (952.5 lb), with a sloping splinter shield. The L/42 barrel imparted a muzzle velocity of 762 m/sec (2,500 ft/sec) to the 0.7 kg (1.5 lb) solid armour-piercing shot, which gave a maximum range of 4,025 m (4,400 yd), although the effective anti-tank range was only 500 m (547 yd). At this range the gun was capable of pentrating 48 mm (1.89 in) of homogenous armour plate at right angles, 36 mm (1.42 in) if the same armour was sloped at 30° from the vertical (60° from the horizontal). This was only sufficient to dent British and French medium/heavy tanks even in 1940, and was useless except through a lucky flank or rear shot against the even heavier Soviet vehicles encountered in 1941. Indeed, so bad was the situation that the gun was christened 'the Army's door knocker'!

Its life was extended by providing it with tungsten carbide-cored shot, which is heavier and denser than steel. (The effectiveness of a solid armour-piercing round is determined by the equation 0.5 mass x velocity^2, the projectile imparting all its kinetic energy against the smallest possible surface for greatest penetration effect). This 0.354 kg (1.18 lb) shot, designated Panzergranate (Pzgr) 40, was fired at 1,030 m/sec (3,380 ft/sec) and could penetrate 65 mm (2.56 in) of vertical armour or 55 mm (2.16 in) sloped at 30° at the above range. Even later, with the development of hollow-charge anti-tank rounds* in 1942, the gun was issued with a fin-stabilized bomb-shaped round, Stielgranate 41, which fitted into the end of the barrel and was

fired by means of a blank round in the breech, just like a rifle grenade. Although the effective anti-tank range with this weapon was only some 300 m (328 yd), it could penetrate 180 mm (7 in) of armour, more than sufficient to destroy any AFV then in existence.

Because of the inadequacy of the basic Pak 35/36, the 5 cm Pak 38 L/60 which had been designed by Rheinmetall-Borsig in 1938 was rushed into service, beginning to equip the anti-tank battalions of the Army and Waffen-SS late in 1940. This was a much superior weapon and was subsequently retrofitted to many PzKpfw III tanks which had started life with 3.7 cm weapons as well. The Pak 38 weighed 986 kg (2,174 lb) and was of conventional split trail design, with rubber-tyred wheels, a torsion bar sprung carriage and a sloped double splinter shield. The basic round was the Panzergranate 38 which weighed 2.25 kg (4.96 lb) and was fired at a muzzle velocity of 823 m/sec (2,701 ft/sec) to a maximum range of 2,650 m (2,900 yd). However, effective anti-tank range was only half this. At 1,000 m (1,094 yd) the Pzgr 38 round could penetrate 61 mm (2.4 in) of vertical armour, 50 mm (1.97 in) at 30°, while at 500 m (547 yd) the figures were 78 and 61 mm respectively (3 and 2.4 in), just sufficient to inflict serious damage on a Russian T-34 tank. Later a tungsten carbide-cored round was introduced, Pzgr 40; this weighed 0.975 kg (2.15 lb) and was fired at a muzzle velocity of 1,198 m/sec (3,932 ft/sec). Armour penetration at 1,000 and 500 m (1,094 and 547 yd) against vertical and 30° armour respectively was 84/55 mm and 120/86 mm (3.3/2.16 and 4.72/3.38 in). Even later a hollow charge projectile was developed as on the Pak 35/36; this was identical in weight and penetrative capability but effective range was less at 150 m (164 yd). This meant it was actually *less* effective than the tungsten-cored round but, as with aluminium and brass, tungsten was in increasingly short supply as the war progressed, so the hollow charge projectile had to be substituted.

Even while development of the Pak 38 was proceeding, both Krupp and Rheinmetall-Borsig were working independently on an even more powerful 7.5 cm weapon, but no urgency was introduced into the programme until after the invasion of Russia and the first guns were not ready to enter

*Hollow charge, or High Explosive Anti-Tank (HEAT) rounds as they are now known, do not work on kinetic energy so are not reliant upon muzzle velocity for their effect. A cone-shaped explosive charge detonates forwards upon impact, creating a pressure wave of molten plasma which blasts a hole through the armour plate. The size of the explosive charge and the diameter of the warhead determine effectiveness. However, if such rounds spin in flight, as from a rifle barrel, much of their effectiveness is dissipated, so they are stabilized in flight by means of fins as on a rocket. (In more recent years spin-stabilized rounds have been developed but these were unknown in the 1940s.)

service until November 1941. The Rheinmetall design, designated Pak 40, was effectively a scaled-up Pak 38 with the same type of carriage, and subsequently became the most widely-used German anti-tank gun of the War, although it never fully supplanted the Pak 38. It weighed 1,425 kg (3,142 lb) in action, which made it awkward to man-handle in mud or snow or over rough terrain, but its effectiveness could not be denied. The standard anti-tank round (like all German A/T guns, the Pak 40 could also fire high explosive shells) was the Panzergranate Patrone (Pzgr Patr) 39 which weighed 6.8 kg (15 lb). Muzzle velocity was 792 m/sec (2,599 ft/sec) and maximum range 7,680 m (8,402 yd), but maximum effective anti-tank range was only 2,000 m (2,188 yd). At this range armour penetration was 98 mm (3.86 in) against vertical armour, 73 mm (2.87 in) when sloped at 30°; at 1,000 m (1,094 yd) the figures were 121 and 94 mm respectively (4.76/3.7 in) and at 500 m (547 yd) 135 and 106 mm (5.3/4.17 in). As with the Pak

Above *A 5 cm Pak 38 being towed by an SdKfz 10 half-track* (BA 98/652/7a).

Above right *Another Pak 38, this time being towed by a Steyr RSO fully-tracked truck* (BA 240/2130/5).

Right *An apparently successful Pak 38 crew judging by the number of tank 'kill' markings on the barrel* (Christopher Ailsby Historical Archives).

Weapons of the Waffen-SS

Left *Another Pak 38, included because of its unusual winter camouflage scheme* (Fred Stephens).

Below left *Taken on 28 or 29 January 1944 near Sobry Kerkhov, this photo shows the 7.5 cm Pak 40 commanded by Knights Cross winner Sturmann Remi Schrÿnen* (Remi Schrÿnen via Christopher Ailsby).

Right *Even though they have Army-style helmet covers, this Pak 38 crew is actually men of the 5th SS Sturm Brigade, which later evolved into the 28th SS Freiwilligen Division* Wallonien (Christopher Ailsby Historical Archives).

38, a tungsten-cored round was also developed, Pzgr Patr 40. This only weighed 3.2 kg (7 lb) but was fired at 933 m/sec (3,060 ft/sec), giving armour penetration at 2,000, 1,000 and 500 m against vertical and sloped armour respectively of 98/66 mm (3.86/2.6 in), 133/96 mm (5.24/3.78 in) and 154/115 mm (6/4.53 in). The reason its performance was no better than that of Pzgr Patr 39 at extreme range is because of the lighter weight of the round.

Even more effective than the Pak 40 was the rival Krupp design, the Pak 41, a squeeze-bore gun of unusual configuration in that the barrel was not tapered throughout its length but was parallel for the first 2.95 m (9.7 ft), then tapered at one in twenty for 25 cm (9.84 in), one in twelve for 18 cm (7 in), then became parallel again for the final 61 cm (2 ft). This design compressed the 7.5 cm tungsten-cored Pzgr 41 round to 5.5 cm, imparting very high muzzle velocity and a smaller — and hence kinetically more effective — impact area. The barrel was constructed in two halves so that the squeeze part could be unscrewed and replaced when worn, after around 500 shots. Unfortunately, as we have seen earlier, tungsten was in short supply by the end of 1941 and virtually ran out completely by the end of the following year, so only 150 Pak 41s were built. Had it remained in production it would undoubtedly have supplanted the Pak 40 since it was capable of defeating the armour of any known tank.

Other unconventional aspects of its design were that the shield was an integral part of the split trail carriage instead of being bolted on, and the barrel was elevated on a ball mounting. When production of the Pak 41 ceased, some spare carriages were fitted with the Rheinmetall 7.5 cm Pak 40 barrel.

The Pak 41 weighed 1,356 kg (2,990 lb), slightly less than the Pak 40 but not noticeably so to a sweating gunner. The Pzgr 41 round itself weighed only 2.59 kg (5.7 lb) but emerged from the barrel at 1,127 m/sec (3,690 ft/sec), so armour penetration was formidable: 124/102 mm (4.9/4 in) against vertical and 30° armour at 2,000 m (2,188 yd); 177/145 mm (6.97/5.7 in) at 1,000 m (1,094 yd); and 209/171 mm (8.23/6.73 in) at 500 m (547 yd). (Maximum range was around 4,000 m (4,376 yd) but is irrelevant since there was no high explosive round for the Pak 41.)

Of course, tapered bore guns using the Gehrlich principle, in which the full-bore driving band at the rear of the projectile is compressed in the barrel, were not entirely new to the German armed forces, for both 2.8 and 4.2 cm weapons had been introduced earlier in 1941, the first examples going to Rommel in North Africa. Both of these were genuine tapered-bore guns, in that the barrel diameters decreased equally throughout their length. Like the Pak 41, though, they fell into disuse after 1942 because of the shortage of Wolfram from which tungsten is refined.

The 2.8 cm Panzerbüchse 41 was designed as a light infantry weapon and was remarkably successful, weighing only 229 kg (505 lb) and standing a mere 83.8 cm (33 in) in height; the gunner and loader operated lying prone. (An even lighter model without a splinter shield and featuring a tubular steel carriage was also introduced for airborne use; this only weighed 118 kg (260 lb).) The 2.8 cm tungsten-cored Pzgr Patr 41 round, which itself only weighed 0.13 kg (0.29 lb), was squeezed down to 2 cm in the barrel, from which it emerged at a velocity of 1,402 m/sec (4,600 ft/sec). Maximum effective range was 500 m (547 yd), at which armour penetration against vertical and sloped armour was 66 and 52 mm (2.6 and 2 in) respectively.

The 4.2 cm Panzerjägerkanone 41 which also entered production at around the same time had a barrel actually tapering from 4.061 cm to 29.41 cm. This was simply mounted on the carriage of the Pak 35/36. The complete gun weighed 450 kg (992 lb) in action (not 642 kg/1,415 lb as sometimes quoted) and its 0.336 kg (0.74 lb) Pzgr Patr 41 round was fired at a muzzle velocity of 1,265 m/sec (4,150 ft/sec). Armour penetration for such a small calibre weapon was excellent: 60/53 mm (2.36/2.08 in) at 1,000 m (1,094 yd), 87/72 mm (3.42/2.83 in) at 500 m (547 yd). However, material shortages stopped production after only a few of these guns had been produced. They principally saw action in Russia. A projected 7.5 cm tapered bore gun designated Pak 44 never entered production.

Returning to the 7.5 cm class of anti-tank gun, when the Germans first invaded Russia in June 1941 they captured thousands of weapons abandoned by the Red Army, including large quantities

2.8 cm tapered bore anti-tank gun manned by Fallschirmjäger (BA 540/407/17).

of the standard Soviet divisional field gun, the 76.2 mm M1936. These were rebored to take the same ammunition as the Pak 40 and entered German service as the 7.62 cm Pak 36(r) early in 1942. This was an excellent weapon although not quite as good as the Pak 40 when firing Pzgr 39 because its muzzle velocity was lower, 740 m/sec (2,429 ft/sec), even though it was actually *better* with tungsten-cored Pzgr 40, when muzzle velocity went up to 990 m/sec (3,250 ft/sec). Armour penetration at 2,000, 1,000 and 500 m against

vertical and 30° sloped armour respectively was as follows: Pzgr 39 — 87/71 mm (3.42/2.8 in), 108/88 mm (4.25/3.46 in) and 120/98 mm (4.72/3.86 in); Pzgr 40 — 84/55 mm (3.3/2.16 in), 130/92 mm (5.1/3.6 in) and 158/118 mm (6.2/4.64 in). The gun weighed 1,730 kg (3,815 lb), so was heavier than the Pak 40, and was of conventional design with a split trail carriage, rubber-tyred wheels and a bolted-on splinter shield, but being designed in the first place as a field gun it suffered in the anti-tank role because of its extra

height — 1.4 m (4.6 ft) compared with the Pak 40's 1.24 m (4.1 ft).

The next anti-tank gun up the scale started life as an anti-aircraft weapon, and its capabilities in its new role were only discovered by accident by Rommel when he used the weapon to stem a British counter-attack on the 7th 'Ghost' Panzer Division near Arras in 1940. This was, of course, the famous 8.8 cm Flak 18 and '36 (Flak = *Flieger-abwehrkanone* — anti-aircraft gun), the 'eighty-eight' so dreaded by Allied tank crews which in slightly revised form comprised the main armament of the Tiger tank (qv). Its development as an AA weapon is covered separately below. A Krupp design, it first entered service in 1934 and the only significant difference between the '18 and '36 is that the latter model featured barrel liners which could be replaced to extend the weapon's life without changing the entire barrel. The basic design was a mixture of elements from the First World War 8.8 cm anti-aircraft gun, which was mounted on a four-wheeled carriage, and the 7.5

An 8.8 cm Flak 18/36 deployed in the anti-tank role in the Ukraine (BA 78/109/5a).

cm Flak L/60 of the 1920s, which introduced the cruciform platform comprised of carriage and outriggers. When being transported, the two ends of the carriage were connected to two-wheeled 'limbers' and the outrigger arms folded upwards against the sides of the gun. In action, the outriggers were lowered and the limbers removed so that the gun sat flat upon its platform, which had adjustable pads at the end of each arm to compensate for irregularities in the ground surface. As an anti-tank weapon the main defect of the Flak 18/36 was its height, since being designed as an anti-aircraft weapon where high elevation is required it was mounted on a tall central pedestal, and the addition of a splinter shield when its anti-tank capabilities were discovered did not help this, overall height being 2.42 m (7.94 ft).

The '88' could also be fired while still mounted on its wheels, but with reduced accuracy and only in an approximately fore and aft direction. Even so this was still a useful attribute in an ambush situation.

Weighing 4,985 kg (10,992 lb) in action (without limbers, 7,200 kg (15,876 lb) with), the Flak 18/36 fired a 9.4 kg (20.73 lb) armour-piercing shell* at 795 m/sec (2,609 ft/sec) or high explosive at 820 m/sec (2,691 ft/sec), having a maximum horizontal range of 14,680 m (16,060 yd or 9.1 miles) with the latter. In the anti-tank role it was rare for the weapon to be used outside 2,000m, and armour-piercing capabilities at this, 1,000 and 500 m against vertical and 30° sloped plate are as follows: 88/72 mm (3.46/2.83 in), 106/87 mm (4.17/3.42 in) and 117/93 mm (4.6/3.66 in). (It will be noted that these figures are not as good as those for the 7.5 cm Pak 40 for, despite its heavier shell weight, the Flak 18/36 (and '37, which only differed in having two instead of three barrel liners and revised gunlaying equipment) had not been designed specifically as an anti-tank weapon. However, improvements were on the way.)

Following the 1940 campaign in the west it was decided that an anti-tank capability should be built into all future 8.8 cm guns, including the Flak 41 which Rheinmetall put into production in 1941. This fired the same basic rounds as the Flak 18/36/37 but had a longer L/71 barrel (instead of L/56) which gave improved ballistic properties, muzzle velocity rising to 980 m/sec (3,216 ft/sec) with armour-piercing shot, 1,000 m/sec (3,282 ft/sec) with HE, and horizontal range with the latter to 20,000m (21,880 yd or 12.4 miles). Maximum armour penetration accordingly increased to 132, 165 and 185 mm (5.2, 6.5 and 7.3 in) at 2,000, 1,000 and 500m. Overall height of the deployed weapon was also slightly reduced to 2.36 m (7.74 ft).

Meanwhile, Krupp had been giving serious

thought to manufacture of a dedicated 8.8 cm anti-tank gun rather than a dual-purpose weapon and in 1943 came out with the Pak 43. This utilized an L/68 or L/71 barrel with a muzzle brake for the first time and employed the usual cruciform platform but without the high pedestal, reducing overall height to 2.05 m (6.73 ft). A well-sloped splinter shield rather then the vertical one on the Flak weapons helped to achieve this. The same system of fore and aft detachable transport limbers was used, but they were lower-slung and the gun could be fired in all directions while in travelling mode. It was undoubtedly the finest anti-tank gun of the war to go into mass production. Overall weight was 3,700 kg (8,158.5 lb) in action, 5,000 kg (11,025 lb) complete with limbers, a considerable reduction compared with the anti-aircraft guns which greatly aided mobility. The weight of the armour-piercing Pzgr Patr 39/43 round was a kilogram heavier than previously, at 10.4 kg (22.93 lb), and with a muzzle velocity of 1,000 m/sec (3,282 ft/sec) this gave phenomenal armour-piercing ability — at 2,000, 1,000 and 500 m against vertical and sloped armour respectively of: 159/139 mm (6.26/5.47 in), 190/167 mm (7.48/5.47 in) and 207/182 mm (8.15/7.16 in). In at least one engagement, Pak 43s are known to have knocked out Soviet T-34s at 3,500 m range (3,829 yd), a remarkable achievement for the time. This would have been with armour piercing high explosive (APHE) shot rather than solid rounds. (The sighting graticules were marked up to 4,000 m (4,376 yd).) Despite the late date in the War, precious tungsten was also found for a 7.3 kg (16 lb) Pzgr Patr 40/43 round which had even superior performance, being fired at a muzzle velocity of 1,130 m/sec (3,709 ft/sec). Armour penetration to the above specifications was: 184/136 mm (7.24/5.35 in), 241/192 mm (9,49/7.56 in) and 274/226 mm (10.79/8.9 in). The gun could also fire an HE round to a maximum range of 17,500 m (19,145 yd or 10.88 miles).

Because output of Pak 43 barrels exceeded production of the complex cruciform carriage, a large number were mounted on spare leFH 18 split-trail carriages, with and without splinter shields. These were designated Pak 43/41. Performance was identical but weight rose to 4,380 kg (9,658 lb).

The last German anti-tank guns to be built were

*Even before Rommel's experience at Arras, the '88' had been used as an improvised anti-tank gun on a couple of odd occasions during the Spanish Civil War, and a high explosive armour-piercing round put into production as a result, although early in the Second World War only a couple of such rounds would normally be carried in the rear of the SdKfz 7 half-track towing vehicle-cum-ammunition limber. As the gun's versatility became further proven, increasing numbers of A/T rounds were carried. (The SdKfz 7 could actually carry a total mixed load of up to 80 rounds.)

the Krupp and Rheimetall prototypes of a 12.8 cm weapon designated Pak 44. The Luftwaffe had had an anti-aircraft gun of this calibre since 1938 and in 1943 work began to turn this into a dedicated A/T gun, as had been done with the Pak 43. The Krupp design was effectively a scaled-up Pak 43 on the same type of two-wheeled transport limbers fore and aft, featuring a cruciform platform with horizontally folding outriggers and a well-sloped splinter shield. The Rheinmetall design also had a cruciform platform but with two pairs of wheels permanently attached to the front arm of the cross; in action, these folded upwards off the ground. A separate two-wheeled limber was attached to the rear of the gun for transport. Although these would have been more devastating than the Pak 43, firing a shell nearly three times the weight (28.3 kg/62.4 lb) with the ability to penetrate 173 mm (6.8 in) of armour at 3,000 m (3,282 yd), only prototypes had been completed by the war's end and neither design reached the front line, although the same barrel was fitted to the Jagdtiger (qv).

Anti-aircraft guns

The German Army and the Waffen-SS were well-endowed with anti-aircraft (Flak) weapons both towed and mounted on half or fully-tracked chassis. The smallest, designed for use against low-flying fighters and ground-attack aircraft, was the 2 cm Flak 30 which first saw action in Poland in 1939. This quick-firing (280 rpm) gun weighed 483 kg (1,065 lb) and in action rested on a three-legged platform; for transport, the whole assembly was lifted on to a two-wheeled tubular steel trailer. Firing a 0.12 kg (0.26 lb) high explosive, incendiary or armour-piercing shell with a muzzle velocity of 899 m/sec (2,950 ft/sec), it had a vertical range of 2,134 m (7,004 ft). Like all German anti-aircraft guns it could also be deployed against ground targets, when maximum range was 2,697 m (2,950 yd).

After the Polish campaign a gun with a greater rate of fire was requested, and Mauser reworked the design to produce the Flak 38 which could fire 450 rpm. Other characteristics remained unchanged. Then, in 1940 Mauser produced a four-barrelled version on a single mounting for the Navy, which was rapidly adopted by the Army and SS as well as

the 2 cm Flakvierling. The complete weight of this was 1,520 kg (3,352 lb) and the four barrels could hurl out a lethal 1,800 rpm, making it an extremely effective weapon indeed.

Next up the scale was the 3.7 cm Flak 18 introduced in 1935. This weighed 1,757 kg (3,858 lb) and was mounted on a cruciform platform. It had a rate of fire of 160 rpm and its 0.556 kg (1.2 lb) shell could reach a vertical height of 4,785 m (15,704 ft), or 6,492 m (7,100 yd) against ground targets. However, it was considered too heavy and cumbersome so only a few were manufactured before an improved version was introduced, on a three-legged platform with a two-wheeled trailer like the Flak 30/38. This entered service in 1937 as the Flak 36. Overall weight was reduced to 1,544 kg (3,504 lb) but other characteristics were identical to those of the Flak 18. Later in the War, in 1943, a further refined version was introduced, the 3.7 cm Flak 43. This was lighter still at 1,247 kg (2,750 lb) and had a revised system for inserting fresh ammunition clips without upsetting the gunner's aim, and which increased the rate of fire to 250 rpm, but was otherwise no different from the earlier guns. A twin mounting was also built, the 3.7 cm Flakzwilling 43, with the barrels one above the other; this weighed 2,781 kg (6,132 lb) and had a rate of fire of 500 rpm.

Finally, in 1944 Rheinmetall came up with a new 3 cm weapon on the same carriage as the Flak 38 in order to give the light anti-aircraft battalions more punch. Designated Flak 103, this weighed 618 kg (1,363 lb) and fired a 0.15 kg (0.33 lb) shell at a rate of fire of 400 rpm with a muzzle velocity of 899 m/sec (2,950 ft/sec) to a maximum height of 4,694 m (15,406 ft), or to a range of 5,715 m (6,252 yd) against ground targets.

During the late 1930s the need for a gun capable of covering the middle zone between the ranges of the light 2 and 3.7 cm and the larger 8.8 and 10.5 cm weapons was realized, and in November 1940 the 5 cm Flak 41 began entering service. It had a cruciform platform on two pairs of transport axles and a small splinter shield either side of the barrel. Weight in action was 3,100 kg (6,834 lb) and it fired a 2.2 kg (4.85 lb) shell at a rate of 130 rpm. Muzzle velocity was 840 m/sec (2,757 ft/sec) giving vertical and horizontal ranges of 5,600 and 12,400 m (18,379 ft and 13,566 yd). However, it was not a

Above *Gebirgsjäger loading a 2 cm Flak 38* (BA 48a/2261/29a).

Below *A 2 cm Flak 38 deployed in mountainous terrain* (BA 309/815/40).

Left *A 2 cm Flakvierling being towed behind a truck (BA 220/636/22).*

Below *2 cm Flakvierling deployed in the ground role; it was as effective against unarmoured and lightly armoured vehicles as it was against low-flying aircraft (BA 303/586/26).*

Weapons of the Waffen-SS

successful weapon and in 1942 work began on a new 5.5 cm design, the Gerät 58, which was to have been radar-controlled. Due to manufacturing problems only prototypes were produced and it never entered service.

The most famous German anti-aircraft gun of all time is unquestionably the 8.8 cm Flak 18 L/56 and its successors. This owed much to a Krupp design of 1918 which had been mounted on a four-wheeled carriage but had proved rather unstable. The Flak 18 was the result of a collaborative venture between Krupp and Bofors in Sweden, and plans were brought back to Germany in 1931. Prototypes were built in secret but troop trials took place in 1933 after Hitler's rise to power and the gun entered service in the following year. It had a cruciform platform, the outriggers folding upwards when it was being towed on its two two-wheeled transport limbers, the barrel and recoil mechanism being mounted on a tall central pedestal which permitted an elevation of 85°. Weight in action was 4,985 kg (10,992 lb) and the gun fired a 9.4 kg (20.7 lb) shell with a muzzle velocity of 820 m/sec (2,691 ft/sec) at a rate of 15 rounds per minute. Maximum vertical range was 8,000 m (26,256 ft), and the gun's capabilities in the anti-tank role have already been discussed.

After some modifications to the basic design, including simplified construction of the platform and limbers and a new barrel manufactured in three sections, the gun was redesignated the Flak 36 but other characteristics remained unchanged. The same is true of the Flak 37 which came out in 1939 with a two-part barrel and revised gunlaying sights. These three weapons served side by side with distinction throughout the war. By this time, however, the need for an improved weapon with greater range and a faster rate of fire had already been forseen, so Rheinmetall began work on a gun with a longer (L/71) barrel to enhance the muzzle velocity. There were difficulties in producing the barrel, which was originally in three pieces as on the Flak 36, because it was found that the steel cartridge cases jammed in the joint between the first and second sections and would not always eject. A change to brass cases helped but the trouble was not fully resolved until a two-part barrel was made. Other modifications included a new turntable which reduced the height by a shade

from 2.42 to 2.36 m (7.94 to 7.74 ft) even though elevation was actually improved from 85 to 90°.

The 8.8 cm Flak 41 which resulted was a very good weapon which served the German armed forces extremely well for the remainder of the war. Although it weighed more than the earlier series of guns, at 7,800 kg (17,199 lb or 7.7 tons), it had a higher muzzle velocity of 1,000 m/sec (3,280 ft/sec) which increased effective altitude to 9,760 m (32,025 ft), only a fraction under the 10,000 m (32,820 ft) which had originally been specified. Rate of fire also went up to 20 rounds per minute.

Other heavier anti-aircraft guns which existed, such as the 10.5 cm Flak 38/39, and 12.8 cm Flak 40 — which provided the basis for the gun in the Jagdtiger (qv) — were either static or mounted on flatbed railway wagons so do not come into the category used by the Waffen-SS although isolated ones may well have been from time to time. Such ordnance was predominantly the province of the Luftwaffe, though.

Inevitably, various means were adopted to make anti-aircraft guns as mobile as the other units in Panzer and Panzergrenadier formations, particularly later in the war when Allied aerial supremacy began to make itself really felt. However, none of them was manufactured in large quantities and towed guns remained vastly predominant. The first SP AA guns appeared in 1941 when the 2 cm Flak 30 began to be mounted on light SdKfz 10 half track chassis, which was designated SdKfz 10/4. and the Flak 38 on the same vehicle, which was known as SdKfz 10/5. (The 3.7 cm Pak 35/36 and 5 cm Pak 38 anti-tank guns were also mounted on the latter vehicle.) The basic Demag SdKfz 10 Typ D 7 was 4.9-tonne (4.82-ton) vehicle with either an open or a lightly armoured driving cab, overall weight rising to 5.59 tonnes (5.5 tons) with the anti-aircraft gun and crew of six or seven men. It was powered by a six-cylinder 4,170 cc Maybach water-cooled petrol engine which developed 100 bhp at 3,000 rpm, giving a top speed of 65 km/h (40 mph). Fuel capacity was 115 l (25.3 gal), range being 300 km (186 miles) on roads, 170 km (106 miles) cross-country. The vehicle's overall dimensions were length 4.75 m (15.6 ft), width 1.93 m (6.33 ft), and height to top of cab 1.62 m (5.32 ft).

The same gun was also mounted in a lightly-armoured open-topped superstructure on the rear

Left *A Wirbelwind 2 cm Flakvierling in Normandy, summer 1944 (BA 496/3455/9).*

of the PzKpfw 38(t) tank (qv), which in this configuration weighed 10.16 tonnes (10 tons) and had a crew of four.

The 2 cm Flakvierling was similarly mounted on the Krauss-Maffei SdKfz 7 half-track, the standard towing vehicle for the 8.8 cm Flak 18/36/37 and /41 and the Army's and Waffen-SS's principal 10.5 and 15 cm field artillery pieces. The SdKfz 7/1, as it was known in this configuration, weighed 11.176 tonnes (11 tons). It was driven by a six-cylinder 6,191 cc Maybach water-cooled petrol engine which developed 140 bhp at 2,600 rpm for a maximum speed of 50 km/h (31 mph). Fuel capacity was either 213 or 203 l (47-44.66 gal) depending upon the vehicle's date of production, giving an average road range of 250 km (155 miles), 120 km (74.6 miles) cross-country. The vehicle's overall dimensions were length 6.85 m (22.48 ft), width 2.35 m (7.7 ft), and height to top of cab 2.62 m (8.6 ft).

In 1943 the 2 cm Flakvierling was also mounted in a fully-rotating turret on the chassis of the PzKpfw IV tank (qv), when it was known as the Wirbelwind ('Whirlwind'), 105 of which were eventually produced. (A single PzKpfw IV mounting just one 2 cm weapon was built, designated Mobelwagen ('Furniture Van'), but the remaining 240 vehicles of this design had a 3.7 cm weapon.) The Wirbelwind weighed 22 tonnes (21.65 tons), other characteristics being as for late model PzKpfw IVs. The Mobelwagen with a single 3.7 cm Flak 43 appeared at the same time and weighed 25 tonnes (24.6 tons). Instead of a turret, it had four downwards-folding steel doors or flaps on top of the chassis, but these did not provide adequate crew protection, especially when the weapon was being used against ground targets, so a revised design was put into production in 1944 with a turret similar to that on the Wirbelwind. Designated Ostwind ('East Wind'), this weighed the same as the latter and had identical performance. Only 43 were manufactured before the end of the War.

The 3.7 cm Flak was also mounted on the SdKfz 10/5, SdKfz 6/2, SdKfz 7/2 and SdKfz 9/2 half-tracks. The 6/2 was a Büssing-NAG design weighing 8.9 tonnes (8.76 tons) fully-laden. It was powered by a six-cylinder 5,420 cc Maybach HL 54 TUKRM water-cooled petrol engine developing 115 bhp at 2,600 rpm which gave a top speed of 50 km/h (31 mph). Fuel capacity was 190 l (41.8 gal), giving a road range of 310 km (192.6 miles), 150 km (93 miles) cross-country. Overall dimensions were: length 6.235 m (20.46 ft); width 2.26 m (7.4 ft); and height to top of cab 2.5 m (8.2 ft). The much larger SdKfz 9/2, principally a heavy artillery tractor, weighed 18 tonnes (17.7 tons). It was powered by a 10,830 cc Maybach V12 water-cooled petrol engine which developed 250 bhp at 2,600 rpm to give a maximum speed of 50 km/h (31 mph). Fuel capacity was 290 l (63.8 gal), which gave a road range of 240 km (149 miles), 100 km (62 miles) cross-country. Overall dimensions were length 8.25 m (27 ft), width 2.6 m (8.53 ft), and height to the top of the cab 2.85 m (9.35 ft).

The 2 and 3.7 cm weapons were also mounted upon trucks on various occasions, and a prototype of a vehicle comprising a twin 3 cm Flak 103 in a fully-rotating turret upon a PzKpfw IV chassis was also completed, but never entered service. (Named Kugelblitz — 'Lightning Ball' — the latter formed the basis for the design of the post-war American M-42.)

A limited number of 8.8 cm anti-aircraft guns were also mounted on SdKfz 8 and '9 half-tracks, usually with lightly armoured cabs for crew protection. The SdKfz 8 was a 13-15-tonne (12.8-14.8-ton) vehicle depending upon load, manufactured by Daimler-Benz. (All the above German half-tracks were very similar in appearance, apart from their size, regardless of differences in manufacturer.) It was powered by a 8,520 cc Maybach V12 water-cooled petrol engine which developed 185 bhp at 2,500 rpm and gave a road speed of 51 km/h (32 mph). Fuel capacity was 250 l (55 gal) which provided a road range of 250 km (155 miles), 110 km (68 miles) cross-country. Overall dimensions were length 7.35 m (24.1 ft), width 2.5 m (8.2 ft), and height to top of cab 2.77 m (9.1 ft). A projected 8.8 cm Flak on a PzKpfw IV chassis similar to the Hornisse tank destroyer (qv) never went into service.

Mountain guns

The German Army and the Waffen-SS Gerbirgsjäger divisions *Nord, Prinz Eugen, Handschar, Skanderberg* and *Kartsjäger* utilized two basic types of mountain gun during the Second World War, although numbers of the older 7.5 cm Geb K 15 which entered production in 1925 still survived. The latter was a very old-fashioned weapon in appearance, a Skoda design with spoked solid steel wheels, a single trail, short, bulky barrel and large splinter shield. Like all mountain guns it could be disassembled (in this instance into seven separate loads) so as to be carried by men or mules on steep rocky slopes. The basic gun weighed 630 kg (1,389 lb) and fired a 5.47 kg (12 lb) shell with a muzzle velocity of 386 m/sec (1,267 ft/sec) to a maximum range of 6,625 m (7,248 yd).

By the 1930s this weapon was deemed unsatisfactory, and with the German armaments industry back in full swing after Hitler's accession to power in 1936, the Army asked for a new gun which Rheinmetall began manufacturing in 1938. This was the 7.5 cm Geb G 36, a much more modern design with rubber-tyred wheels, split trails and a muzzle brake to reduce recoil and thus lessen the weight of the recoil and recuperative machinery. Weighing 750 kg (1,654 lb) in action, it could be broken down into eight separate loads for transporting. It fired a 5.75 kg (12.68 lb) shell with a muzzle velocity of 475 m/sec (1,559 ft/sec) to a range of 9,150 m (10,010 yd). In 1942 an improved version, lighter and more stable, was designed by Böhler, but only four prototypes of the 7.5 cm Geb G 43, as it was designated, were made and it never went into production.

Largest of the mountain guns was the 10.5 cm Geb H 40, another product of the Austrian Böhler company which entered service in 1942. It was another split trail design weighing 1,660 kg (3,660 lb) which could be broken down into five separate loads. It fired a 14.5 kg (32 lb) shell with a muzzle velocity of 565 m/sec (1,854 ft/sec) to a maximum range of 16,740 m (18,314 yd). A projected 15 cm mountain gun from the same company never went beyond prototype stage because by this period of the war the Gebirgsjäger had found that recoilless guns originally designed for airborne operations were more suited to their needs.

Above *Manhandling a 7.5 cm GebG 36 through snow must have been a pretty exhausting task. There was provision to mount the carriage of this gun on skis* (BA 99/719/21a).

Above right *A 7.5 cm GebG 36 deployed for action* (BA 100/781/9).

Right *A dismantled GebG 36 being loaded on to horses* (BA 102/882/26a).

Recoilless guns

When Rheinmetall began experimenting with recoilless guns at the beginning of the 1930s they gave them the cover name 'leichte Geschützen' (light guns) to conceal their real character. This name persisted even after there was no longer need for secrecy and the first production weapon, which was manufactured by Krupp as well as Rheinmetall, entered service as the 7.5 cm LG 40 in 1941. It had a short L/18 barrel with a Laval-type venturi through which the propellant counter-charge was exhausted, either with a sliding block breech (Rheinmetall model) or swing breech (Krupp model). The former had a light tubular metal carriage on motor cycle wheels, the latter using aircraft tailwheels. In both cases there were two towing trails and a barrel clamp, the latter folding

down to form the third leg of a tripod when the wheels were removed for action. The LG 40 weighed a mere 145 kg (320 lb) in action and fired a 5.8 kg (12.79 kg) shell at a muzzle velocity of 350 m/sec (1,149 ft/sec) to a range of 6,800 m (7,439 yd).

In the same year, 1941, Krupp and Rheinmetall introduced larger 10.5 cm versions of the same weapon, the former being designated LG 40 and the latter lG 42. Apart from the firing mechanism, which was above the barrel instead of in the breech to save unecessary erosion, they were very similar to the smaller gun. The Krupp LG 40 weighed 388 kg (855.5 lb), the Rheinmetall LG 42 540 kg (1.191 lb). Both fired a 14.8 kg (32.6 lb) shell to a range of 7,950 m (8,697 yd), but the LG 42 had a longer barrel (L/17.5 instead of L/13) which gave a higher

Above *Gebirgsjäger with a recoilless 10.5 cm LG 40 gun* (BA 103/927/2).

Opposite *Although these are Luftwaffe paratroopers, the pictures are included to show further examples of the LG 40 being towed by an NSU Kettenkraftrad half-tracked motor cycle and deployed in action* (BA 543/562/22 and 570/1616/17a).

muzzle velocity (835 m/sec or 2,740 ft/sec instead of 335 m/sec or 1,099 ft/sec) and thus made a more effective anti-tank weapon, although this was not its primary role. As with all recoilless weapons, their main disadvantage was the violent backblast which could not only endanger friendly troops but also gave the gun's position away to the enemy every time it fired. The usual towing vehicle for all recoilless weapons was the NSU Kettenkraftrad, or half-tracked motor cycle.

Rocket artillery

Rockets are almost certainly the oldest form of artillery, being used by the Chinese centuries before the invention of cannon in the early middle ages, and today the ripple-launch multiple rocket system is a very important area in the armouries of all the world's major armies. This was not always so, and William Congreve's attempts to revive the rocket in the British Army during the Napoleonic Wars met with very limited success. This remained true throughout the nineteenth and early twentieth centuries, and it is ironic that it was the Treaty of Versailles at the end of the First World War that spurred on the German Army to develop the first effective modern systems — designated Nebelwerfer, or 'fog-thrower', to disguise their true purpose. This came about because, along with all the many other restrictions discussed elsewhere, the Reichswehr was forbidden to develop new heavy artillery pieces. However, nowhere did the Treaty mention rockets.

Main picture *Nebelwerfers firing at night* (BA 216/449/16a).

Inset *Setting up a Nebelwerfer in an Italian field* (BA 304/643/15).

Above *An Opel Maultier armoured half-track with ten 15 cm Nebelwerfer tubes* (BA 689/190/30).

Below *Loading the Nebelwerfer tubes on the same vehicle* (BA 689/190/27).

An experimental team was set up at Kummersdorf under General Walter Dornberger to investigate the possibilities. One of the problems with earlier rockets was that having the propellant charge at the rear produced in-flight instability as the fuel burnt away, making them grossly erratic and inaccurate. Dornberger's team came up with the then-revolutionary idea of putting the propellant at the front of the rocket, exhausting through venturis towards the rear — which is where the high explosive charge was placed. By angling the venturis, they could also be used to impart spin to the missile, further stabilizing it and enhancing range and accuracy. The result was a brilliant success and entered service in Russia in 1941 as the 15 cm Nebelwerfer or Wurfgerät ('appliance caster') 41. The 15 cm missiles were 930 mm (36.6 in) long and weighed a total of 34.1 kg (75.2 lb), the actual warhead being 10 kg (22 lb) of high explosive. They were loaded into the rear of six barrels or launching tubes constructed in a circular frame on the carriage of the obsolete 3.7 cm Pak 35/36 anti-tank gun. The warhead was fired electrically by means of a remote-control cable, since the crew needed to retire at least 15 m (16.4 yd) to protect themselves from the rockets' formidable blast. The rockets were discharged in a ripple salvo at two-second intervals and had a maximum range of 6,700 m (7,330 yd). Landing close together, they had a devastating effect against dense troop or vehicle concentrations and could severely damage heavy AFVs. (The Nebelwerfer could also live up to its cover name by firing smoke shells to provide a blanket smokescreen.) Later in the war a special self-propelled 15 cm Nebelwerfer vehicle was developed, ten tubes being mounted in two layers on a swivelling mount on the fully-armoured rear body of an Opel Maultier half-track.

The weapon proved so successful that there were immediate demands for a more powerful version, and these resulted in the Wurfgranäte 42. This was a 21 cm weapon but due to wartime exigencies less time could be devoted to development than had been the case with the earlier design, so it ended up with a conventional layout — warhead at the front and rocket at the rear. This meant it was far less accurate but since the Red Army persisted in mass

attacks of almost suicidal nature, the Germans were not over-worried. The WGr 42 round weighed 112.5 kg (248 lb) overall, the warhead being 47.2 kg (104 lb). It was 1,250 mm (49.2 in) long and had a range of 7,850 m (8,588 yd). Meanwhile, experiments had also been carried out with the 32 cm Wurfkörper Flamm ('flame container thrower'), a single-shot incendiary rocket which had entered service at approximately the same time as the Nebelwerfer 41. This was a large and inaccurate missile, 1,300 mm (51.2 in) long and weighing 78.4 kg (172.8 lb), with a limited range of only 2,200 m (2,407 yd). It was fired from an open-sided steel crate. To supplement this a new 28 cm high explosive rocket was designed, also with the propellant in the tail and the warhead at the front, which could be launched from the same open launching racks. These racks were then fitted three a side to SdKfz 251 armoured half-tracks to make them more mobile and give their crews some protection, the system being designated 28/32 cm Nebelwerfer 41 to show its dual calibre nature. The 28 cm missile was exactly the same length as the 21 cm WGr 42 (and, indeed, the latter weapon could be fired from the same launching racks if internal guide rails were fitted). The complete weight was 83.7 kg (184.5 lb) of which 61 kg (134.5 lb) represented the warhead, but again range was short at only 1,925 m (2,106 yd).

The final development in German rocket artillery was the 30 cm Wurfkörper Spreng ('explosive container thrower') which could be fired from the same launch racks as the 28/32 cm Nebelwerfer 41, either mounted on half-tracks or in 'six-packs' on an artillery carriage. This had a greatly enhanced range of 4,550 m (4,978 yd) but was still inaccurate. It was 1,240 mm (48.8 in) long and weighed 125.6 kg (277 lb), of which 66.33 kg (146.2 lb) was warhead.

All these pieces of ordnance had high explosive warheads whose principal characteristic was blast, although there was some shrapnel from the casing and rocket. They were not armour piercing but a direct hit would severely concuss the crew of the heaviest tank, so they were widely used in helping break up large enemy armoured formations, as well as against buildings and infantry in the open.

An SdKfz 251 armoured half-track fitted with launching racks of 28/32 cm rockets. This is actually an Army not an SS vehicle, of the 8th Panzer Division (BA 208/21/39a).

4. Armoured cars

The Germans made extensive use of armoured cars throughout the war and had developed a number of standard types for reconnaissance and more specialized roles since the mid-1920s. The first criterion was for a heavy vehicle and from this emerged the six-wheeled SdKfz 231 series which entered production in 1930, 928 vehicles being manufactured over the next six years by Mercedes-Benz, Büssing-NAG and Magirus. This was followed by the light four-wheeled SdKfz 221 series produced by Horch, 2,118 of which were manufactured between 1935 and 1942. The third series was eight-wheeled but, confusingly, also designated SdKfz 231. This Büssing-NAG design stayed in production from 1937 to 1942, 1,235 being manufactured, after which a superior vehicle, the SdKfz 234, entered service, with approximately 1,000 being made between 1943 and January 1945.

Two particularly interesting characteristics of the eight-wheeled German cars were the fact that the wheelbase was designed so as to allow them to run on railway tracks with the tyres removed from the wheels; and the provision of two driving positions, one at the front and one at the rear. Although the latter feature (which was shared by the four-wheeled SdKfz 221 series) was principally designed for rail travel, it was doubtless a comfort to many crews who got themselves into a tight spot. The light armoured cars were four-wheel drive, the six-wheeled variants were driven by the rear two pairs of wheels and the eight-wheeled variants had independent drive to each wheel which meant they could still function even if two wheels on each side

were knocked off or damaged.

The first car to go into production was the 5 tonne (4.92 ton) Mercedes SdKfz 231 6x4 which was powered by a six-cylinder Daimler-Benz M 09 water-cooled petrol engine of 3,663 cc developing 65 bhp at 2,900 rpm; this was followed from 1932 by the Büssing-NAG utilizing a four-cylinder 3,920 cc water-cooled petrol engine of their own design, the Type G, which developed 60 bhp at 2,500 rpm; and finally from 1934 by the slightly heavier (5.3 tonne/5.2 ton) Magirus variant which again used a power plant of their own design, the S 88 six-cylinder 4,562 cc water-cooled petrol engine which developed 70 bhp at 2,200 rpm. All shared similar performance, being capable of 65 km/h (40 mph). The Mercedes variant carried 105 l (23.1 gal) of fuel and the Magirus 110 l (24.2 gal), giving them both a road range of 300 km (186.4 miles), 200 km (124.3 miles) cross-country; the Büssing-NAG design only carried 90 l (19.8 gal) and range was reduced to 260 km (161.6 miles) on roads, 140 km (87 miles) cross-country.

The basic SdKfz 231 carried a crew of four and was armed with a 2 cm KwK in a small fully-traversing turret; the SdKfz 232 was identical apart from the provision of extra radio equipment and a large overhead frame aerial; the SdKfz 233 was turretless and mounted a 7.5 cm StuK L/24 in an open-topped fighting compartment, while the SdKfz 263 was again turretless but had an armoured superstructure and frame aerial and could carry an extra man. Dimensions of the SdKfz 231 were length 5.57 m (18.3 ft), width 1.82 m (5.97 ft),

Above *An SdKfz 221 light armoured car* (BA 275/558/15).

Left *Another view of the same type of vehicle. Note SS number plate* (BA 159/109/7).

Above right *SdKfz 232 eight-wheeled armoured car with frame radio aerial; this vehicle belonged to the* Wiking *Division.*

and height 2.9 m (9.52 ft). Frontal armour was 14.5 mm (0.57 in), sides and rear 8 mm (0.31 in).

Next into production from 1935 to 1940 was the four-wheeled 3.75 tonne (3.69 ton) SdKfz 221 Ausf A. This compact car was powered by a Horch V8 water-cooled petrol engine of 3,517 cc (3,823 cc in the Ausf B) which developed 75 bhp at 3,600 rpm (81 bhp Ausf B), giving a road speed of 75-80 km/h (46.6-49.7 mph). Fuel capacity was 100 l (22 gal) with a road range of 280 km (174 miles), 200 km (124.3 miles) cross-country. The crew was two men and basic armament just a single machine-gun, although a 2 cm KwK or 2.8 cm sPzB and an extra man was accommodated in the SdKfz 222, a 2 cm KwK and a third man in the '223 radio vehicle, and four men in the unarmed and turretless SdKfz 260/261 radio vehicles. Armour thickness was as on the SdKfz 231 and overall dimensions of the '221 were length 4.8 m (15.75 ft), width 1.95 m (6.4 ft), and height 2.06 m (6.76 ft). (It should be noted that vehicle weight varied according to equipment and number of crew and could be as high as 4.8 tonnes (4.72 tons), but without any significant effect upon performance.)

The third series was the eight-wheeled Büssing-NAG SdKfz 231 and variants. The early (1937-38) and late (1939-42) products had slightly different V8 water-cooled petrol engines, both given the designation Typ L8V-GS, the former of 7,913 cc producing 150 bhp at 3,000 rpm, the latter of 8,360 cc giving 180 bhp at the same revs, but overall weight (8.3 tonnes/8.17 tons) and speed (85 kmh (52.8 mph)) were identical. Fuel capacity was 150 l (33 gal) giving a road range of 300 km (186.4 miles), 160 km (100 miles) cross-country. This armoured car again was produced in several variants: the '231 had a crew of four and a 2 cm KwK in a fully-revolving turret; the '232 (weighing 8.8 tonnes (8.66 tons)) was the same, plus a frame radio aerial; the '233 (8.58 tonnes (8.44 tons)) was turretless and had a 7.5 cm StuK in an open-topped fighting compartment; and the '263 (8.4 tonnes (8.26 tons)) had a crew of five and extra radio equipment in a spacious armoured superstructure.

Although these designations are confusing since they are the same as for the 6x4 cars, the vehicles can easily be identified pictorially and most books suffix the SdKfz numbers with (6-rad) or (8-rad) according to the number of wheels. (Greater confusion exists between visual identification of the SdKfz 231 (8-rad) and the SdKfz 234 which succeeded it, but the simplest means in most instances is that the former had two sets of mudguards each side, each embracing two wheels, whereas the latter had a single staggered mudguard the full length of the vehicle covering all four. A well-known plastic construction kit manufacturer did not realize this a few years ago, resulting in a model of a vehicle which never existed and which has provided hours of joy to 'kit bashers' (conversion enthusiasts) ever since!)

Basic dimensions of the SdKfz 231 (8-rad) were length 5.85 m (19.2 ft), width 2.2 m (7.22 ft), and height 2.34 m (7.68 ft), although the latter went down to 2.25 m (7.38 ft) on the '233 and up to 2.9 m (9.52 ft) on the '232 and '263. Armour thickness was 14.5 mm (0.57 in) frontally on the early production vehicles, 30 mm (1.18 in) later, and 8 mm (0.31 in) around the sides and rear.

While the SdKfz 231 was a useful vehicle, by 1942 something better was needed and Büssing-NAG came up with their Typ ARK, especially designed to operate in the extreme climatic conditions of Russia, which entered service the following year as the SdKfz 234 and was again produced in several variants. It was considerably heavier at 11.7 tonnes (11.5 tons) so a correspondingly more powerful 12 cylinder 14,825 cc Tatra 103 air-cooled diesel engine was installed which produced 210 bhp at 2,200 rpm for a very respectable 90 km/h (56 mph). The '234 was outwardly similar to the '231 apart from the mudguards as noted above, although there were numerous detail differences and overall dimensions were larger. The '234 carried 240 l (52.8 gal) of diesel fuel as standard, but this could be increased to 360 l (79.2 gal) in the turretless versions, giving a road range of 6-900 km (373-559 miles), 4-600 km (248-373 miles) cross-country.

The size of the basic '234 was length 6 m (19.7 ft), width 2.33 m (7.65 ft), and height 2.1 m (6.9 ft), although the latter increased to 2.38 m (7.8 ft) on the SdKfz 234/2 'Puma' and to 2.35 m (7.7 ft) on the SdKfz 234/3 and /4. The original vehicle was simply armed with a 2 cm KwK as on the earlier '231 but on the '234/2 Puma a long-barrelled 5 cm KwK L/60 was introduced in a fully-revolving turret, and this armoured car is widely regarded as the best produced by any nationality during the war, having a very effective anti-tank capability and the speed to get itself close to the enemy rapidly and then out of trouble again. The '234/3 and /4 were open-topped variants, the former with the venerable 7.5 cm StuK L/24 and the latter with the excellent 7.5 cm KwK L/48 as fitted to late versions of the PzKpfw IV tank (qv). There was no dedicated radio-command variant of the SdKfz 234. Armour thickness on all versions was the same as for late SdKfz 231 (8-rad)s, but increased to 14.5 mm (0.57 in) at the rear to help protect the engine.

All of the above vehicles were used by the Waffen-SS formations but in the early days, during the latter part of the French campaign in 1940 as well as in Greece and during the first year in Russia, the stringencies on equipment procurement which hampered their growth meant that they made extensive use of captured French Panhard 4x4 armoured cars, which were not issued with a *Sond-*

erkraftfahrzeug (SdKfz) number but designated sPz Spähwagen Typ 178 bzw P 204 (f). These were excellent, well-rounded 8.3 tonne (8.17 ton) vehicles driven by 6,330 cc Panhard water-cooled Typ ISK petrol engines which developed 105 bhp at 2,000 rpm, giving a top speed of 72.5 km/h (45 mph). The Waffen-SS acquired approximately 190 of them. The 150 l (33 gal) of fuel carried gave a road range of 350 km (217.5 miles), 210 km (130.5 miles) cross-country. Crew was four men and main armament a 2.5 cm quick-firing gun. Overall dimensions were length 5.14 m (16.87 ft), width 2.01 m (6.6 ft), and height 2.36 m (7.74 ft). Armour thickness ranged from 20 mm (0.79 in) frontally to 7 mm (0.27 in) at the sides and rear. Like all

captured vehicles impressed into German service, these Panhards usually had larger-than-normal black and white (or white outline) crosses prominently painted on them.

To assist the armoured cars in their primary role of reconnaissance, armoured half-tracks (see next chapter) and motor cycles, which could be armed with a machine-gun in a sidecar, were also used, so they deserve brief mention. There are too many types to enumerate in detail, but the principal ones were the little 125 cc DKW RT 125 (which was not 'man' enough for a sidecar, but stayed in production throughout the war), the 350 cc BMW 'Victoria' KR 35 WH which was in production from 1938 right through to 1945, and the 750 cc BMW R

BMW R75 motor cycle combination with a crudely-whitewashed Tiger in the background (BA 279/946/20).

75 and Zündapp KS 750 which were manufactured from 1940 to 1944. (Others used in smaller quantities included the 250 cc NSU 251 OS, 350 cc BMW R 35 and DKW NZ 350, 400 cc BMW R 4, 500 cc Zündapp K 500 W, 600 cc Zündapp KS 600 W and NSU 601 OSL, and the 800 cc Zündapp K 800 W. Captured British Triumph BD Ws were also popular!)

The 350 cc BMW was a single-cylinder four-stroke

Left Despatch rider wearing the special rubberized motor cycle coat on a 350 cc DKW; note Kar 98 slung across his back (BA 297/1743/21).

developing 14 bhp at 4,000 rpm capable of 100 km/h (62 mph), and its 14 l (3 gal) fuel tank gave it a range of 400 km (248 miles). The 750 cc BMW R 75, the best-known German bike of the war, had a twin-cylinder four-stroke engine producing 26 bhp at 4,400 rpm and was capable of 92 km/h (57 mph) with sidecar. Its 24 l (5.28 gal) tank gave a range of 340 km (211 miles). The Zündapp had a slightly larger engine (actually 751 cc compared to 746) but virtually the same power output of 26 bhp at 4,000 rpm. Top speed was 95 km/h (59 mph) and the 23 l (5.06 gal) of petrol carried gave a range of 330 km (205 miles). Its usual weapon was an MG 34 or '42.

5. Tanks and armoured fighting vehicles

As we have seen earlier, the Army was parsimonious in allocating modern weapons to the Waffen-SS, and this was especially true of tanks until the three premier divisions (Leibstandarte *Adolf Hitler, Das Reich* and *Totenkopf*) were elevated to Panzergrenadier formations for the spring 1943 counter-offensive in Russia, each with an integral tank battalion. These changes were authorized during January – May 1942 but not implemented until between August and November. (The fourth of the crack divisions, *Wiking*, was also allocated a tank battalion, but instead of being withdrawn to France to re-equip, stayed in the line while it received its tanks.) There were many reasons for these developments, including Hitler's and Himmler's determination to maintain the elite status of the fighting SS divisions, but the build-up in their strength in 1943 was undoubtedly accelerated by Rommel's defeat at El Alamein in November 1942, by the Allied landings in Tunisia the same month (Operation 'Torch') and by the encirclement of Paulus's VI Army at Stalingrad. Equally important was the recall to active duty of General Heinz Guderian as Inspector-General of Armoured Troops on 28 February 1943. (Guderian, the principal architect of the German Panzer force pre-war, had been dismissed by Hitler on 26 December 1941 following a row on the 20th during which the General had vigorously opposed the Führer's plans for the conduct of the war in the east following the failure to capture Moscow.)

Guderian was given complete independence of the OKH and OKW and was made directly responsible to Hitler alone; his duties embraced all aspects of recruitment, training, organization and equipment for the Panzer divisions, both Army *and* Waffen-SS. His most urgent concern at this time was with equipment, for over the preceding year Hitler, labouring under the misguided impression that it was he alone who had salvaged the Army from defeat during the winter of 1941 – 42, had placed ever-increasing emphasis on production of assault guns (principally defensive weapons) to the detriment of tank manufacture*. Moreover, the bulk of these weapons were allocated to artillery rather than Panzer formations. Guderian soon changed things and established a cordial working relationship with Albert Speer, who had succeeded Fritz Todt as Armaments Minister when the latter was killed in a plane crash on 8 February 1942.

A paraphrase of Guderian's observations and priorities at the stage of the war, given in full at a conference in Vinnitsa presided over by Hitler on 9 March 1943, sheds a great deal of light on the problems he had uncovered during his initial few days in this new post.

---

*See accompanying tables of representative tank and SPG production figures. Nearly twice as many assault guns and tank destroyers were built during the year preceding Guderian's appointment than were tanks. The following year shows a much more balanced picture even though overall production is down due to the mounting effectiveness of the Anglo-American strategic bombing campaign.

German tank production

Model	1934-39	1939-40	1940-41	1941-42	1942-43	1943-44	1944-45
PzKpfw I	c 2,500						
PzKpfw II	c 900	625 (1939-43)					
PzKpfw II Luchs				131 (to 1943)			
PzKpfw 35 (t)	c 300						
PzKpfw 38 (t)		c 1,500 (1938-42)					
PzKpfw III	95	c 1,500	c 1,400	c 1,900	760		
PzKpfw IV	467	150	1,724 (to 1942)		3,073	3,800 (to 1945)	
PzKpfw V Panther					534	1,768	3,740
PzKpfw VI Tiger I					1,355 (to 1944)		
PzKpfw VI Tiger II							487
Totals	4,262	3,775	3,124	2,031	5,722	5,568	4,227

German assault gun and tank destroyer production*

Model	1934-39	1939-40	1940-41	1941-42	1942-43	1943-44	1944-45
4.7 Pak (t) auf Pz IB		132					
7.62 Pak (r) auf Pz II (Marder II)				150	185		
7.5 Pak 40 auf Pz II (Marder II)					531		
7.62 Pak (r) auf Pz 38 (t)					344		
7.5 Pak 40 auf Pz 38 (t)					418	381	
Panzerjäger 38 (t) Hetzer						1,577 (to 1945)	
StuG III A-E			734				
StuG III F/G					7,900 (to 1945)		
StuG IV					c 1,500		
Jagdpanzer IV L/48						c 1,500	
Jagdpanzer IV L/70							c 300
8.8 cm Pak auf III/IV Hornisse (Nashorn)						493	
Jagdpanther							382
Elefant (Ferdinand)					90		
Jagdtiger							74
Totals		132	734		10,968	3,951	756

*Excluding second-line vehicles built on captured French chassis and self-propelled artillery.

Weapons effectiveness: an Allied Sherman used as a target showing the penetrative ability of the Tiger's 8.8 cm gun, the Panther's 7.5 cm and the PzKpfw III's 5 cm L/60 (BA 313/1004/21).

First was a realization that the prior practice of creating extra Panzer divisions in name but not equipping them fully nor even keeping the existing divisions up to strength (nominally 400 tanks) had to cease. It was far more important, Guderian stated, to keep a smaller number of divisions at peak efficiency than to maintain a larger number of inadequate formations in the field. (Unfortunately, the earlier practice continued until the War's end, and Hitler fell into the trap of authorizing the establishment of new divisions — particularly SS ones — and then treating them as if they really existed, whereas towards the end most in reality were ragtag collections of youths and old men with obsolete or poorly reconditioned weapons, of battalion or regimental size rather than divisions!)

The existing Panzer divisions, Guderian observed, were far from being kept up to strength, but the whole point of the structure he had originally created was that these divisions should be balanced bodies of all arms working interdependently. If there was a shortfall in the number of tanks available, therefore, the division would be imbalanced and unable to fulfil the tasks allotted to it and expected of it. Then, noting the fact that German tank production was only adequate to equip one tank battalion a month (and that each division had, in theory, four Panzer battalions), he tried to persuade the conference that the assault guns being manufactured in such quantities should be assigned to armoured instead of artillery formations as a stop-gap measure until the new Tigers and even newer Panthers were in full production. On this particular point, however, he was overruled.

Guderian also called for far more thorough testing of new equipment and training of its users before it was committed to action. (The first Tigers unwisely thrown into the battle around Leningrad for propaganda reasons had suffered from inept leadership and unsuitable terrain, leading to a minor disaster and the capture by the Russians of several of the German Army's latest AFVs.) Furthermore, he laid down that no new weapon should in future be committed to battle until it had been properly proven and, equally importantly, was available in sufficient quantity to be decisive. (This was a forlorn hope, as events proved.)

Another section in which Guderian attacked prior practice was in the allocation of new vehicles to non-profitable sideshows of the war rather than where the main action was (ie, Russia). He always denied that this observation was aimed at Rommel, but many German officers shared the misguided opinion that the Army's effort was wasted in North Africa. It is interesting to speculate on whether the presence of an SS division in the desert might have spurred greater efforts to keep the Afrika Korps supplied as it needed to be and should have been.

One of the problems the Germans shared with most other nations, including Britain (who did not solve it until the Centurion went into production right at the war's end), America (who resolved it with the Sherman) and Russia (who solved it earliest with the T-34) was a multiplicity of tank and assault gun designs from a variety of manufacturers. (The PzKpfw I was made principally by Henschel and MAN but Wegmann was a sub-contractor on the Ausf B, while Daimler-Benz and Alkett made the command, anti-tank and artillery versions; the PzKpfw II was a MAN design but also produced by Henschel, Famo and Daimler-Benz, with Alkett joining in again on some of the SP versions; the PzKpfw III was a Daimler-Benz design with variants also being produced by Alkett and MAN; the PzKpfw IV was Krupp's, but Steyr, Vomag, Praga and Deutsche Eisenwerke also manufactured variants; the Panther was an MAN product but MNH, Daimler-Benz, Henschel, Miag and Demag were also involved; the Tiger was the result of a competition between Henschel and Porsche, but by the time the contract eventually went to the former Porsche had already completed 90 chassis, so these were turned into heavy assault guns originally called Ferdinand (after Professor Porsche) and subsequently re-christened Elefant; a similar situation arose between the two firms with the Tiger II, and as a result the first 50 had a Porsche-built turret.)

Kenneth Macksey has observed (*Panzer Division: The Mailed Fist*, Purnell 1968) that 'Up to 1942, demands on industry to produce equipment always came as an order from the High Command, each Service fostering certain factories which worked exclusively for them... with the result that, at a time when Germany suffered shortage in capacity as well as many items, several factories did not receive sufficient orders to keep them in full employment when their branch of the service had run short of demands... there were confusions over the supply of spares mixed with sudden demands for improvements to old marks of tank at the moment when new ones were being rushed from prototype straight into production... From lack of effective central direction, the most dreadful confusion permeated the German tank industry in 1942.' It was this confusion which Guderian and Speer had to work together to eliminate, and one of the reasons why Guderian's brief included the Waffen-SS as well as the Army was to eliminate the 'private industry' which the SS had created in the face of the Army's intransigence over the supply of modern equipment. The irony is that from this point onwards, the premier Waffen-SS divisions began receiving priority in the allocation of new tanks and SPGs, and eventually the seven full-fledged SS Panzer divisions which emerged during 1943-44 had a stronger tank establishment than their Army equivalents (50 + per battalion instead of 50 −) and also got the new Tigers and Panthers more promptly despite their short supply.

During the first six months of 1942, when the four premier SS divisions were turned from motorized into Panzergrenadier divisions, the principal tanks in production were the PzKpfw III Ausf J and the PzKpfw IV Ausf F2 and G. When the Panzer divisions were first being organized under Guderian in the mid-1930s the basic idea was that the Army needed three types of tank — a light reconnaissance machine (PzKpfw II), a medium tank armed with a high velocity gun to combat enemy tanks (the PzKpfw III) and a support tank armed with a larger calibre gun of lower velocity firing high explosive rounds to take out enemy anti-tank guns, machine-gun positions and the like. By 1942 the inadequacy of the PzKpfw II had been well proven and production was being tapered off, but one company (nominally 22 tanks) in each of the SS Panzer battalions was equipped with PzKpfw IIFs.

The IIF was a 9.5 tonne (9.35 ton) vehicle driven by a Maybach HL 62 TRM six-cylinder water-cooled petrol engine of 6,191 cc capacity, producing

Above *A line-up of PzKpfw IIs seen through a hatch in another vehicle* (BA 78/3076/22a).

Below *PzKpfw IIIJ fitted with spaced frontal armour and hull skirts, accompanied by PzKpfw IVs* (BA 689/195/3).

Weapons of the Waffen-SS

Two contrasting views of PzKpfw IIIMs during the summer of 1943 with and without spaced armour on the gun mantlet (BA 219/595/23 and 19).

Above *PzKpfw IIIs with 5 cm guns cross a frozen river. In the background can be seen 2 cm Flakvierling anti-aircraft guns mounted on half-track chassis* (BA 218/544/19).

Below *PzKpfw IIIs with short 5 cm L/42 guns* (BA 218/504/26).

Opposite *PzKpfw IIIs in difficult terrain in the Balkans* (BA 162/256/39 and 166/515/22).

Tanks and armoured fighting vehicles

Main photograph *Late-production PzKpfw IIIL without escape hatches in the lower hull sides and with spaced armour. Note the aerial recognition flag draped across the engine plates of the vehicle in the background and the use of logs to cross a boggy patch of ground* (BA 78/3076/10a).

Inset left *An early production PzKpfw IIIL which still has the hull escape hatches but also the new turret introduced on this variant without side vision ports* (BA 78/3075/4).

Inset right *Infantry armed with Kar 98s follow a StuG III* (BA 78/3083/39).

Left *PzKpfw IIIJ with 5 cm L/60 gun photographed in southern Russia* (BA 215/398/36a).

Below *PzKpfw III with 5 cm L/60 gun alongside a StuG III with 7.5 cm weapon in a* saukopf *mantlet, both* Wiking *Division vehicles* (BA 78/22/1).

Right *In the spring, thaw logs had to be used frequently to help tanks traverse soft ground, as with this PzKpfw III (Christopher Ailsby Historical Archives).*

Below right *Once out of the mud, the going was still often pretty terrible. These are* Wiking *Division PzKpfw IIIs (Christopher Ailsby Historical Archives).*

Weapons of the Waffen-SS

140 bhp at 2,600 rpm and giving a top road speed of 40 km/h (25 mph). It carried 170 l (37.4 gal) of fuel in two tanks which gave a road range of 150 km (93 miles), 100 km (62 miles) cross-country. The tank had a crew of three and was armed with a 2 cm KwK 38 L/55 recoil-operated quick-firing gun with a cyclic rate of 420-480 rpm and a muzzle velocity of 800 m/sec (2,625 ft/sec), plus a co-axial 7.92 mm MG 34 machine-gun. The main armament was useless against enemy tanks but its high rate of fire made it lethal against light armoured reconnaissance vehicles, armoured half-tracks and the like. Dimensions of the PzKpfw IIF were length 4.81 m (15.8 ft), width 2.28 m (7.5 ft) and height 2.02 m (6.6 ft). Frontal armour was 30-35 mm thick (1.2-1.4 in), sides and rear 14.5-20 mm (0.6-0.78 in). Its five roadwheels on their leaf-spring suspension gave adequate cross-country performance, although its tracks were rather narrow so it suffered over soft or muddy ground.

The PzKpfw IIIJ was one of the last in this long line of vehicles, production of which had started in 1936. It weighed 22.3 tonnes (21.9 tons) and was powered by a Maybach HL 120 V-12 water-cooled

Things were better in the summer months. Here a PzKpfw III races past an SdKfz 251 half-track manned by SS grenadiers during the battle of Kursk. The gun is an MG 42 (BA 81/143/4a).

petrol engine of 11,867 cc which produced 300 bhp at 3,300 rpm, giving a road speed of 40 km/h (25 mph). It carried 320 l (70.4 gal) of fuel giving a road range of 140 km (87 miles), 90 km (56 miles) cross-country. The PzKpfw IIIJ had a crew of five and was armed with a 5 cm KwK L/42 or L/60 main gun plus one co-axial and one bow 7.92 mm MG 34 machine-gun, the latter in a ball mounting (earlier PzKpfw IIIs had a 'letterbox' mount).

The L/60 gun which was fitted to all except the earliest few PzKpfw IIIJs was a very effective semi-automatic weapon which could be fired up to 12 to 14 times a minute (under ideal conditions, of course; under field conditions it was more like 8-10). It had a muzzle velocity of 823 m/sec (2,700 ft/sec) and its 2.22 kg (4.9 lb) standard round could penetrate 78 mm (3 in) of homogenous armour plate at 90° at 457 m (500 yd) or

61 mm (2.4 in) at 1,000 m (1,094 yd). Against sloped armour (typical 60°) it was, of course, less effective, but could still penetrate 47 and 40 mm respectively (1.85 and 1.57 in) at the above ranges.

The tank's dimensions were: length 5.56 m (18.2 ft), width 2.95 m (9.68 ft), and height 2.5 m (8.2 ft). Frontal armour was basically 50 mm (2 in) with an extra 20 mm (0.75 in) bolted on, sides and rear being 30 mm (1.2 in). It featured the revised torsion bar suspension first introduced on the Ausf E, with six roadwheels and three return rollers. Like the PzKpfw II (and IV) its tracks were too narrow for its weight so mobility suffered unless the going was firm and dry.

The PzKpfw IVF2 was the first tank in this series to be fitted with a long-barrelled 7.5 cm gun, the first 300-odd having the old short KwK L/24 and being retrospectively designated F1. It weighed 23.6 tonnes (23.2 tons) and was powered by the

PzKpfw IVs advance across the Russian steppes. The foreground vehicle is an Ausf F2, first vehicle in the series to have a long-barrelled 7.5 cm gun (BA 216/413/21).

same engine as the PzKpfw IIIJ which gave it identical speed and cross-country performance since there was only a ton difference in their weights. However, it carried 470 l (103.4 gal) of petrol giving a road range of 190 km (118 miles), 130 km (81 miles) cross-country. The tank had a crew of five and for main armament the 7.5 cm KwK 40 L/43 gun, coupled to a co-axial and bow machine-gun again. Hitherto this weapon had only been fitted to assault guns but the addition of a single ring muzzle brake meant that its recoil could be sufficiently absorbed for it to be fitted into a PzKpfw IV turret (on the L/48 version fitted to the PzKpfw IVH and J a double baffle was required, but some F2s were also retrospectively fitted with these so it does not provide automatic recognition).

The KwK 40 was badly needed since the Germans had encountered the Soviet KV-1 and T-34 with their powerful 7.62 mm weapons;

indeed, the need for such a weapon had been foreseen earlier but nothing was done about it until the Panzers found they were drastically outgunned. Even so the L/43 was no real match for the Soviet gun and even the L/48 was no great improvement, and it was not until the L/70 version emerged on the Panther that something better than parity was achieved. The L/42 and L/48 fired a 6.8 kg (15 lb) projectile at muzzle velocities of 740 and 750 m/sec (2,428 and 2,461 ft/sec) respectively, giving a penetration of 89-100 mm (3.5-3.9 in) of homogenous armour plate at 60° at 457 m (500 yd). This was thus the first German tank gun to be able to hole the T-34's 60 mm (2.36 in) frontal armour at normal combat ranges.

Dimensions of the PzKpfw IVF2 (and G) were length 5.93 m (19.46 ft), width 2.88 m (9.45 ft) and height 2.68 m (8.79 ft). Armour, which was bolted on rather than welded as on the later Tiger

Main picture *Late model PzKpfw IVs with hull and turret side skirts to defeat HEAT rounds, winter 1943/44 (BA 277/843/3).*

Inset *In bleak Russian weather, a StuF III and PzKpfw IVF2 move out (BA 235/962/7a).*

Weapons of the Waffen-SS

Above left *Cleaning the barrel of a PzKpfw IVG of the 3rd SS Panzer Division* Totenkopf, *summer 1943* (BA 219/561A/15).

Left *PzKpfw IVGs ford a Russian stream* (BA 87/3680/9).

Above *Panzergrenadiers hitch a ride on a StuG III* (BA 89/3779/32a).

Above *A whitewashed PzKpfw IVH moves past infantry also camouflaged for winter warfare (BA 277/843/8).*

Left *A captured Soviet T-34/76 with prominent German markings to prevent attack by friendly troops (BA 213/296/5).*

Weapons of the Waffen-SS

and Panther, and therefore weaker, varied from 80 mm (3.15 in) on the turret front and 50 mm (1.97 in) on the hull front to 20 mm (0.79 in) on sides and rear (increased to 30 mm (1.18 in) on the sides of the Ausf G, which was basically the same vehicle as stated except for the double muzzle baffle and L/48 gun). The tank had four pairs of roadwheels per side on leaf-spring suspension and four return rollers; from the start of the F series the tracks were widened from 360 to 400 mm (14.2 to 15.75 in), giving superior cross-country performance to earlier models.

The PzKpfw IV was the only German tank to stay in production throughout the War, and since it was now equipped with an effective anti-tank gun it swapped roles with the PzKpfw III, the latter becoming the support tank from 1942 armed with the short-barrelled 7.5 cm KwK L/24 gun which had equipped earlier Mark IVs. These benefited from the development of hollow charge anti-tank ammunition, which does not rely upon muzzle velocity for its effectiveness. (This innovation, in fact, was another reason why Hitler had switched attention from tanks to assault guns and tank destroyers, for he reasoned — falsely, like so many before and since — that the new weapon fore-shadowed the end of the tank as a decisive battle-field factor.) This PzKpfw III was the Ausf N, which had slightly reduced range (130 km or 81 miles) due to its weight going up to 23 tonnes (22.6 tons), but other factors were unaffected. The PzKpfw IIIL was merely a J with extra armour (5 mm side skirts and a turret ring to deflect hollow charge projectiles, the simple answer to Hitler's fears), while the M was simply fitted with deep wading equipment specifically to cross Russian rivers. (In fact this equipment had originally been designed for Operation 'Sealion', the planned invasion of Britain in 1940 which never came about.)

Further developments to the PzKpfw IV were the Ausf H which had spaced armour as on the PzKpfw IIIL (but many earlier vehicles were also retrofitted with this when they went into workshops for over-haul or repair), and the J, which sacrificed the power traverse for the turret in exchange for extra fuel stowage (680 l or 150 gal) to give greater range (270 km or 168 miles on roads, 180 km or 112 miles cross-country). The power traverse itself was replaced by a simple two-gear manual system. Other detail differences included the removal of vision slits to simplify manufacture and a reduction in the number of return rollers from four to three. Despite the penalty of a weight increase to 25 tonnes (24.6 tons), speed was only marginally reduced to 38 km/h (23.6 mph).

The PzKpfw IV was the Wehrmacht's and Waffen-SS's standard and most widely-used tank throughout the war because its spacious internal layout and general soundness of design allowed it to be progressively upgraded and upgunned to meet changing circumstances. However, it suffered through being thinly armoured for its size despite the later additions, and had the vertical, or nearly vertical, slab-sided appearance which characterized all early German tanks — including the Tiger I. That would change with the PzKpfw V Panther but since the Tiger went into production first I will describe it in chronological order. (There was, incidentally, an earlier PzKpfw V, an unwieldy triple-turreted design produced pre-war; three examples were shipped to Oslo during the Norwegian campaign for propaganda purposes, but it never saw action... for which its seven-man crews were undoubtedly grateful!)

The Tiger is by far the best-known German tank of the war so, alongside the Panther, it deserves special attention.

On the morning of 13 June 1944 a small force of four Tiger tanks of *schwere SS Panzer Abteilung 101 (sSSPzAbt 101),* accompanied by a solitary PzKpfw IV, circumvented a column of the British 7th Armoured Division moving out of Villers-Bocage in the direction of Caen, and hid in a wood. One of their number entered the town itself, where it rapidly knocked out three Cromwell cruiser tanks. A fourth escaped by reversing rapidly into a side street, out of sight. The solitary Tiger continued down the hill through the town but round a corner ran into a whole squadron of Cromwells accompanied by at least one Sherman Firefly, which fired and hit the German vehicle. In the face of this opposition the Tiger turned and retraced its path, coming face to face with the surviving Cromwell from the first engagement. Although the Tiger sustained two further hits it was undamaged and eliminated the enemy in its path before leaving the town to rejoin its comrades.

Above *A Tiger crewman despondently surveys the task of repairing his vehicle's damaged track. Note* zimmerit *paste again applied to the hull* (BA 311/904/23a).

Below *Rear end view of a similar problem* (BA 310/898/25).

Above right *In this view of a third Tiger in a similar predicament the rear idler wheel has been removed for repair or replacement as well. Note the storage rack on the lower hull front for spare track links, some of which have been removed to effect repairs* (BA 22/2948/8).

Right *Contrast this view of a 'clean' Tiger without either* zimmerit *or spare track links with the previous views* (BA 22/2936/17a).

Tanks and armoured fighting vehicles

Above *A crudely whitewashed Tiger in Russia* (BA 218/546/4a).

Below *Tigers closed down for action* (BA 278/885/24a).

This small force then fell upon the squadron they had earlier bypassed and wiped it out, destroying some 25 British AFVs.

The German commander in the lead tank during this attack was SS Obersturmführer Michael Wittmann, the leading tank 'ace' of the Second World War, who had already knocked out 117 tanks and self-propelled guns on the Russian front before being transferred to Normandy. For this engagement he was promoted to Hauptsturmführer and awarded the Swords to the Knights Cross with Oakleaves he had already won.

By 1944 the Tiger was a real 'bogey' to the western Allies, who had first encountered it in Tunisia in 1943, and in contemporary British and American accounts all German tanks are invariably referred to as Tigers, even though most of them were PzKpfw IVs!

The Tiger's origins go back to 1937 when the German Armaments Ministry had issued a specification for a new heavy tank to Daimler-Benz, Henschel, MAN and Porsche. However, this was shelved when the new PzKpfw III and IV proved satisfactory and was not revived until the spring of 1941. Hitler had been impressed by the heavy French Char B1 *bis* and British Matilda I during the French campaign and, with plans well advanced for his assault on Russia, in May 1941 issued a requirement for a tank in the 45-tonne (44.3-ton) class mounting a modified 8.8 cm anti-aircraft gun. Prototypes were to be available for demonstration on his birthday the following year, 20 April 1942.

Henschel and Porsche both commenced work on the VK.4501, as the prototype was code-numbered (VK = *Volkettenfahrzeuge* or fully-tracked experimental vehicle; '45' shows that the tank was supposed to be in the 45 tonne (44.28 ton) class, and '01' that it was the first design to this specification), immediately and the two prototypes were duly shown to Hitler at Rastenburg on the appropriate date. The Henschel design was adjudged marginally superior and went into production in August under the designation SdKfz 181 PzKpfw VI Tiger Ausf H (the latter being changed to Ausf E in February 1944). By this time it was badly needed because the PzKpfw III and IV

had proven inadequate in the face of the Soviet T-34 and KV-1, whose intrinsic superior qualities in 1941 had only been overcome by better German training, tactics and communications.

Before the comparative trials between the two VK.4501 prototypes however, Porsche had already produced 90 chassis for their own design and to avoid waste these were converted into tank destroyers mounting an 8.8 cm PaK 43 gun in a fixed armoured superstructure on the hull rear. These entered service on the Russian front in spring 1943 and were originally named SdKfz 184 Ferdinand, after Dr Ferdinand Porsche, but their crews christened them 'Elefants' because of their size and it was the latter name which stuck. They proved to be rather more of white elephants since they were slow and unwieldy, and although they were effective when they could stand off and engage targets at long range, they were very vulnerable to enemy infantry. (As a sop to Professor Porsche's pride, the name he had chosen for his prototype — Tiger — was applied to the Henschel vehicle!)

Production of the Tiger progressed initially at the rate of 12 vehicles a month, but by November 1942 this had been increased to 25. The Army wanted to hold back introduction of the new vehicle for the spring 1943 offensive, but Hitler ordered it rushed into service and the first few vehicles saw action in Russia in the same month that production commenced — with disastrous results, as mentioned earlier. Advancing in single file over boggy terrain, they were engaged from the flank by concealed Soviet anti-tank guns and either wiped out or abandoned.

Tigers continued to serve on all fronts throughout the remainder of the War, production reaching a peak of 104 in April 1944 and ceasing in August of that year after 1,355 vehicles had been made. By this time the PzKpfw V Panther — a much superior design which could also be manufactured in half the time — was in full scale production and the PzKpfw VI Königstiger (Tiger II or King Tiger) was entering service. The Tiger I proved an invaluable interim design, though, its crews appreciating both its thick armour which was virtually invulnerable frontally to all Allied tank and anti-tank guns despite its slab-sided nature, and its 8.8 cm weapon which could knock out any Allied vehicle. However, it was underpowered and mechanically unreliable, and its slow turret traverse speed made it vulnerable to surprise attacks from the flank. Despite these shortcomings it was regarded with fear and respect by its opponents.

The Tiger I went through various modifications to meet changing demands in the two years it was in production, early versions having an escape hatch in the turret side which was later eliminated, as well as smoke dischargers which were also dispensed with, while vehicles sent to serve in Africa and southern Russian had special air filters against sand and dust. A more powerful engine was installed after 250 vehicles had been produced, and specialized variants included the Sturmtiger and Bergetiger, the former mounting a massive mortar in a fixed superstructure for street fighting and attacking prepared fortifications after German experience at Stalingrad in particular had shown the need for such a vehicle; the latter was an engineer repair and recovery vehicle.

The original Tiger I Ausf H was powered by a Maybach HL 210 P 45 V-12 water-cooled petrol engine of 21,353 cc which produced 650 bhp at 3,000 rpm; later models had the HL 230 P 45 model of the same engine which had a capacity of 23,880 cc producing an extra 50 bhp at the same revs. Maximum speed with either engine only differed by 1 km/h (0.62 mph) from 37 to 38 km/h (23-24 mph) but the extra power available in the 'beefed-up' variant gave slightly greater reliability and cross-country performance. The tank eventually emerged as considerably heavier than originally planned due to the weight of the massive Krupp turret deemed necessary to house the 8.8 cm gun: 56.9 tonnes (56 tons) instead of 45. This was one of the main reasons for its lack of speed and manoeuvrability. It carried 534 l (117.5 gal) of fuel in four compartments, giving a road range of only 100 km (Ausf H) to 117 km (Ausf E) (62-73 miles), a mere 60-67 km (37-42 miles) cross-country. The latter factor made it far more of a defensive weapon, deploying to allow the enemy tanks to approach and then using its powerful gun to knock them off at long range, than an offensive vehicle designed for rapid Blitzkrieg advances.

Like most German tanks, the Tiger I had a crew of five. What made it so formidable was the choice of an 8.8 cm gun as its main armament, a decision dictated by Hitler after the standard German anti-aircraft weapon of the same calibre had proved itself such a brilliant tank killer under Rommel's inspired leadership in France in 1940. At the time of its introduction and for some considerable time afterwards the KwK 36 L/56 was the most powerful tank gun in service anywhere in the world. It fired a 9.4 kg (20.75 lb) armour-piercing shell at a muzzle velocity of 810 m/sec (2,657 ft/sec) which enabled it to pierce 110 mm (4.33 in) of homogenous armour plate sloped at 60° at 457 m (500 yd), a vital 10 per cent improvement over the 7.5 cm KwK 40 L/48. Up to 92 rounds of ammunition could be carried in side stowage bins, beneath the floor and anywhere else handy, including the gunner's lap. The Tiger also had the usual co-axial and bow machine-gun, and a third could be fitted to the commander's cupola for light anti-aircraft defence.

Basic dimensions of the Tiger I were: length 6.3 m (20.67 ft), width 3.55-3.73 m* (11.65-12.24 ft) and height 2.88 m (9.45 ft) Armour protection was 110 mm (4.33 in) on the turret front, 100 mm (3.94 in) on the hull front and 60-80 mm (2.36-3.15 in) sides and rear; the weakest point (the roof) at 26 mm (1.1 in) was as strong as the frontal armour of many 1939 tanks! The Tiger had interleaved and overlocking roadwheels mounted on torsion bar suspension which was strong and gave a stable ride, but the system gave the crews enormous headaches if an inner roadwheel was damaged (by a mine, say) and had to be changed in the field.

The Tiger was principally allocated to independent Panzer battalions of the Army and Waffen-SS rather than to the Panzer divisions, being used at Corps or Army level to reinforce other units during particularly critical operations. The main units were sPzAbt 501-510 and sSSPzAbt 101-103, the former being Army and the latter

---

* With or without trackguards. Because the Tiger was too wide to fit on the standard German flatbed railcars, each was issued with two sets of tracks; one narrow (52 cm/20.47 in) for rail transport and one wide (72.5 cm/28.54 in) for combat.

A Tiger entrained for the front; note the narrow tracks which had to be fitted for rail travel (BA 220/630A/24a).

Waffen-SS formations. In addition the Army's élite *Großdeutschland* and *Panzer Lehr* Divisions had organic Tiger battalions, while the 1st, 2nd and 3rd SS Panzer Divisons Leibstandarte *Adolf Hitler, Das Reich* and *Totenkopf* had integral companies from 1943. Some of the independent battalions were later attached to particular divisions on a semi-permanent basis, such as *sSSPzAbt 503* which became part of the 11th SS Panzergrenadier Division *Nordland**.

Even when the Tiger I was barely in production, Porsche — rankled that their design had been

* For details of the SS Panzer Divisions' histories and organization I would refer readers to my earlier book *Hitler's Teutonic Knights*, also published by Patrick Stephens Ltd.

turned down in favour of the Henschel one — had started work on a successor, designated VK.4502 even though its weight would be far more than the Tiger I's original specification or even its final weight. It was intended to be even more heavily armoured and to mount a longer-barrelled version of the 8.8 cm gun to give greater range and muzzle velocity. However, like their Tiger I design, it suffered from a complicated and expensive engine and transmission system reliant upon materials which the war had rendered rare, and at the beginning of 1943 Henschel were asked to come up with a more competitive design. This they succeeded in doing with the VK.4503, but only after Porsche had gone ahead for the second time and produced 50 turrets for their own tank! As a result the first 50 SdKfz 182 Königstigers had Porsche turrets, the remainder of the production run of 487 having Henschel turrets.

The Tiger II shared many design features with the highly successful Panther, especially in the sloped shape of its hull which was designed to deflect armour-piercing shot. It also had the same engine, which was fine so far as industrial standardization went, but which gave it a hideously low power-to-weight ratio with correspondingly poor mobility and high breakdown rate. By this stage in the War, though, the Wehrmacht was largely on the defensive so speed and the need to sustain a prolonged drive were less essential. Thus, although conceived as an offensive weapon to break the deadlock on the eastern front and resume the German advance, the Tiger II in practice only helped to stem the Allied advance. The same is true of the Jagdtiger tank destroyer (qv), which was essentially a Königstiger with a fixed superstructure in place of the turret to accommodate the formidable 12.8 cm Pak 44. Only 74 were produced during 1944-45, ranking it alongside the earlier and equally unsuccessful Elefant.

First, however, we must look at the Panther, arguably the best tank of the War although that accolade is usually given to the Russian T-34, and it is erroneously stated in many places that the Panther was actually a copy of the latter. That is certainly not true for a specification for a tank in the same class had been issued as early as 1937. As with the Tiger, however, work had been stopped on this when it seemed that the PzKpfw III and IV looked as though they were going to be satisfactory, and was only *resumed* after first clashes with the Soviet vehicle had shown up the deficiencies in their designs.

Towards the end of 1941 Guderian ordered a commission to report on the T-34 and Daimler-Benz and MAN (Maschinenfabrik Augsberg-Nürnberg) were both asked to produce prototypes of a new German tank in the 30 tonne (29.5 ton) class. In an amazingly short space of time, the two VK.3002 prototypes were ready for Hitler's birthday in April 1942. The DB design was almost an exact copy of the T-34, down to the inclusion of a diesel engine, the MB 507. However, while the two prototypes were being produced Hitler had ordered that the planned 7.5 cm L/48 gun should be replaced by an L/70, and it turned out that the turret of the Daimler design could not accommodate this. For that reason, plus fears about the

reliability of the untried diesel engine, Speer and Guderian recommended adoption of the MAN design, which had a turret based upon one of the VK.4501 (Tiger) prototypes sufficiently large to accept the longer gun.

The revised MAN prototype was ready by September 1942 but it already far exceeded the specified 30 tonne requirement, partly because of the new and heavier gun and turret, and partly because Hitler had ordered the frontal armour to be increased from 60 mm (2.36 in, the same as on the T-34) to 80 mm (3.15 in). The PzKpfw V Ausf D, as the first production model was designated, actually weighed in at 44 tonnes (43.3 tons), and the engine with which it was originally to be fitted, the Maybach HL 210, had to be replaced by the more powerful HL 230 P30 V-12 water-cooled petrol engine of 23,880 cc which produced 700 bhp at 3,000 rpm. This gave a useful road speed of 46 km/h (28.6 mph) and the torsion bar suspension coupled with overlapping roadwheels and wide tracks (66 cm or 26 in) gifted the vehicle with better cross-country mobility than any previous German design. (Wide tracks, it should be noted, were another feature copied from the T-34, whose over-snow capability during the winter of 1941-42 had quite demoralized the Panzer crews.)

The Panther carried 730 l (161 gal) of petrol in five tanks which gave a road range of 170 km (105.6 miles), 85 km (53 miles) cross-country; performance was even better on the later Ausf A and G models, 185 km (115 miles) by road or 100 km (62 miles) cross-country. The Panther had a crew of five and, as noted above, was armed with the excellent 7.5 cm KwK 42 L/70 which fired a 6.8 kg (15 lb) round at 934 m/sec (3,063 ft/sec), enabling it to penetrate 141 mm (5.55 in) of homogenous armour plate sloped at 60° at 457 m (500 yd) range — a better performance, it should be noted, than that of the 8.8 cm KwK 36 fitted to the Tiger despite the smaller calibre and shell weight. Seventy-nine rounds of ammunition were carried. There was a co-axial machine-gun but no fixed hull mounting on the Ausf D, although there was a small 'letterbox' flap through which the radio operator could fire if necessary.

The main difference in appearance between the Panther and all preceding German tanks was

Above *A PzKpfw V Panther Ausf D with early-pattern cupola finished in an interesting colour scheme of dark green and/or red-brown over its basic dark yellow finish* (BA 705/264/1).

obvious at first sight: the glacis plate, hull and turret sides and turret rear were all sloped at angles designed to deflect enemy shots, so that although its armour was thinner than that of the Tiger, it was equally effective and, indeed, could not be penetrated at normal combat ranges by any Allied tank until the introduction of the Soviet JS series in 1944. Actual thicknesses were turret and hull front 80 mm (3.15 in), turret sides 45 mm (1.77 in), hull sides and rear 40 mm (1.57 in); on the second production model, the Ausf A, the turret front was increased to 110 mm (4.33 in), but this was reduced back to 100 mm (3.94 in) on the definitive. Ausf. G, while hull sides were increased to the same thickness as those of the turret. Overall

dimensions of all Panther variants were the same, length 6.87 m (22.55 ft), width 3.27 m (10.73 ft) and height 2.95 m (9.68 ft).

The Panther Ausf D entered production in January 1943 but 'our problem child', as Guderian called it, suffered from numerous mechanical teething troubles and all the first batch had to be recalled to the factory for modifications in April. Most were resolved quite simply but throughout its life the Panther's gearbox proved to be its weakest point, and since it took two 18 tonne (17.7 ton) half-tracks to tow a Panther, a specialized armoured engineer and recovery vehicle had to be produced. Known as the Bergepanther, this was simply a turretless Panther with a small wooden

A well-camouflaged PzKpfw V Panther with zimmerit covering: this ceramic paste was widely applied to vehicles in Russia in particular to defeat magnet hand-held anti-tank mines (BA 477/2124/4 and 6).

Two views of an early PzKpfw VA with the improved commander's cupola and driver's vision episcopes but still with letterbox machine-gun flap instead of the ball mounting introduced later in this series (BA 313/1001/32 and 35).

A column of PzKpfw VAs with, in the foreground, a little Borgward SdKfz 301 Ladungsträger, or tracked demolition charge layer (BA 311/940/15 and 18).

First Panther variant was the Ausf D (above left) and the differences between it and the final Ausf G can clearly be seen in these three photographs (BA 88/3746A/27, 280/1096/15 and 12).

Above *A well-camouflaged Panther, possibly photographed in Italy* (BA 281/1104/32).

Right *Engine change for a Panther. The crane vehicle is an SdKfz 9/2 half-track* (BA 280/1096/34).

Infantry carrying boxes of ammunition for an MG 34 or 42 alongside a zimmerit-*finished Panther Ausf G*
(BA 695/408/29).

box superstructure to protect the crew from the elements, a powerful winch and two hydraulically-operated spades at the rear which it could dig in to give itself more traction while hauling a distressed tank out of a muddy ditch. The Panther eventually went into action during Operation 'Citadel', the battle of Kursk, in July 1943; the 1st Panzer Division was the first recipient, followed quickly by the Leibstandarte *Adolf Hitler* and *Das Reich*.

Field experience brought several suggestions for modifications from the troops in the field and these were incorporated in the Ausf A, which had thicker turret armour as noted above, strengthened suspension and a ball-mounted machine-gun in the glacis plate, while episcopes replaced the direct vision slits in the commander's cupola. As a result of these modifications, overall weight went up to 45.5 tonnes (44.77 tons). On the final model, the Ausf G, which went into production in March 1944, further improvements were made to the transmission, the driver's vision slit was replaced by an episcope and extra armour was added to the upper hull sides to give greater protection to the fuel tanks. Ammunition stowage was increased to 82 rounds. The Ausf G was slightly lighter than the A, though still heavier than the D at 44.8 tonnes (44.08 tons).

In battle the Panther proved itself the best German tank of the war, superior to the T-34 even when the latter was upgunned with an 85 mm weapon and far better than any British or American design. Except at really point-blank range it could only be knocked out by a shot from the flank or the rear and it was well liked by its crews. Waffen-SS Panther companies were supposed to be 22 strong compared with 17 in Army formations, but this was not always the case. In February 1944 for example, the strength of each of SS Panzer Regiment 5 *Wiking's* Abteilungen was 76 tanks and SPGs. The 1st Abteilung (battalion) had three companies of 17 PzKpfw IVHs and one company of 17 StuG IIIs plus 8 PzKpfw IVs in the headquarters company, while the 2nd Abteilung had four companies of 17 Panthers plus 8 in the headquarters company. In addition there were 8 further Panthers in the Regimental staff company.

German tanks, incidentally, were numbered by a very simple system which makes identification extremely easy. Regimental staff vehicles were numbered 01 to 08, the number being prefixed by the letter 'R'. Battalion headquarters vehicles were similarly numbered, the numerals being prefixed by a 'I' or 'II' for 1st or 2nd Abteilung. The eight other companies had the numerals 1 to 8 as the first digit, followed by 00 and 01 in the case of the two company headquarters tanks, the numbers 1, 2 or 3 to denote the troop within each company and 1 to 5 to denote the individual tank within the troop. Thus R00 would be the regimental commander's vehicle; I00 that of the commander of the 1st Abteilung and II00 that of the 2nd. The numbers 100 and 101 would be the headquarters tanks of the 1st Company, 1st Abteilung; 111 to 115 the tanks of the 1st Troop, 121 to 125 the second troop and 131 to 135 the third, right up to 835, the fifth tank of the third troop of the eight company. This system was applied to both Army and Waffen-SS vehicles.

With the Tiger in production and the Panther about to commence, Speer began to give thought to an even more powerful tank and in January 1943 issued a specification to Henschel and Porsche. The rival prototypes, designated VK.4502(P) and VK.4503(H) were ready by October, and Porsche were so confident that they had even put their turret design into production. Once again, however, they were to be disappointed as noted earlier

for the Henschel vehicle won the trials and went into production at the end of December.

The PzKpfw VI Ausf B, alias Tiger II alias Königstiger (King or Royal Tiger) was the most powerful tank in the world until the Russians came up with the JS-3 just before the War's end. However, it was badly underpowered since the same Maybach HL 230 P30 engine as in the Tiger I was used despite the fact that the Tiger II weighed 68 tonnes (66.9 tons)! This gave an abysmal power-to-weight ratio and although maximum road speed attained during trials was 41.5 km/h (25.8 mph), any vehicle would have broken down within a couple of kilometres if it attempted to sustain this. However, by the time the tank started to reach the battalions in February 1944 the Germans were on the defensive everywhere so heavy armour and as powerful a gun as possible were far more relevant than mobility.

The Tiger II carried 860 l (189 gal) of petrol in seven tanks giving a road range of 170 km (105.6 miles), 120 km (74.6 miles) cross-country. As with the Panther and Tiger it had a crew of five but its most formidable feature was its 8.8 cm KwK 43 L/71 gun. Designed specifically as an anti-tank gun (whereas the weapon in the Tiger I was an adaptation of an anti-aircraft one), it fired a 10 kg (22.25 lb) round at 1,018 m/sec (3,340 ft/sec) which gave it phenomenal armour penetration — 182 mm (7.16 in) at 60° at 914 m (1,000 yd) and even a substantial 150 mm (5.9 in) at twice that range. The number of rounds of ammunition carried varied from 72 in the Porsche-turreted version to 84 in the Henschel. There was also a co-axial machine-gun and one in a ball mount in the glacis.

The Tiger II shared many features of the Panther, overlapped but not interleaved road-wheels, wide tracks (80 cm or 31.5 in) and similarly-sloped armour to help deflect enemy shot. The armour itself was almost thick enough without this assistance: turret front 180 mm (7 in) and sides 80 mm (3.15 in) — the same as the Panther's frontal hull armour, note; glacis 150 mm (5.9 in); and hull sides and rear also 80 mm. Overall dimensions were length 7.26 m (23.83 ft), width 3.62 m (11.88 to 12.3 ft) depending upon whether combat tracks and side skirts were fitted or whether the vehicle was 'clean' for rail travel; and height 3.07 or 3.09 m (10-10.14 ft) with Porsche and Henschel turret respectively. (The Porsche turret was actually the better of the two designs, although more cramped internally, having a curved front face and better general deflective properties.)

The Tiger II equipped *sSSPzAbt 101*, Wittmann's old unit, from September 1944; re-named *sSSPaAbt 501*, it took part in the Ardennes offensive; *sSSPzAbt 102* was similarly re-equipped at around the same time, renumbered *502*, and destroyed defending Berlin; *sSSPzAbt 103* was re-equipped and renumbered *503* in October 1944 and surrendered after being decimated in East Prussia in May 1945. There were 37 Tiger IIs to each SS battalion.

Assault guns and tank destroyers

As early as 1936 the need for mobile and preferably armoured artillery pieces to support the infantry formations, particularly the motorized divisions, had been foreseen, and this was borne out in Poland in 1939. As a result the StuG III Ausf A (StuG — *Sturmgeschütz*) was put into production in January 1940, and 30 vehicles were available to take part in the closing stages of the French campaign later that summer. Unlike some German self-propelled weapons which were hastily impro-vised designs on obsolete or captured chassis, and frequently used captured guns as well, the StuG III was a purpose-built vehicle. The chassis was that of the PzKpfz III, and on to this was built a low-slung armoured superstructure with a 7.5 cm StuK L/24 gun in the front. (This was identical to the KwK L/24 in the PzKpfw IV; StuK = *Sturmgeschütz Kanone*, KwK = *Kampfwagen Kanone*). The vehicle weighed slightly less than the PzKpfw IIIFs, Gs and Hs in simultaneous production at 19.6 tonnes (19.3 tons) compared with 20.3 to 21.6 tonnes (20-21.25 tons) but speed of 40 km/h (25 mph) and cross-country mobility were identical. The same amount of fuel — 320 1 (70.4 gal) — was carried, giving a road range of 160 km (100 miles), 100 km (62 miles) cross-country. The vehicle had a crew of four and 54 rounds of high explosive amm-

Russian cossacks of the Waffen-SS alongside a StuG III
(BA 31/2437/29).

A StuG III advances through a burning Russian village, late 1942 (BA 275/583/31a).

unition were carried for the main gun, which did not have an effective anti-tank capability.

The StuG III's dimensions were length 5.38 m (17.66 ft), width 2.92 m (9.58 ft), and height 1.95 m (4.45 ft). Frontal armour on the Ausf A was 50 mm (1.97 in) thick, sides and rear were 30 mm (1.18 in). The B, C, and D models which followed were basically identical apart from improvements to the transmission and minor changes to the superstructure which made it 10 cm (0.4 in) longer and higher. The Ausf E which came out in 1941 had a slightly revised internal layout, but even as this was being put into production, experience on the Russian front had shown the need for a more powerful gun with an anti-tank capability, so the Ausf F, manufacture of which commenced in March 1942, mounted either the 7.5 cm L/43 or L/48, again as in contemporary PzKpfw IVs. The revised superstructure needed to accommodate either one of these (or the 10.5 cm StuH L/28 (H = *Haubitze* — howitzer) which was fitted to some StuGs as an alternative), again increasing the vehicle's length and height to 5.56 m (18.25 ft) and 2.15 m (7.05 ft) respectively. (Performance data for these weapons are given above.)

In 1942 the final variant emerged, known as the Ausf G. Nearly 8,000 were produced by the end of the war even though production was adversely affected by a heavy bombing raid on the Alkett factory in 1943. This machine weighed more than earlier versions at 23.9 tonnes (23.5 tons) – 24.5 tonnes (24.1 tons) with the 10.5 cm howitzer — through being up-armoured frontally to 70 mm (2.75 in), having a revised cast (instead of welded) mantlet (the *Saukopf* or boar's head) and side skirts to protect the running gear from hollow charge projectiles. Other factors were unaffected. After the PzKpfw IV and SdKfz 251 half-track (qv), the StuG III was the most common armoured fighting vehicle in German wartime service.

Initially artillery battalions in the motorized divisions were equipped with it and later it formed a major component of the Panzer and Panzergrenadier divisions, when Guderian finally got his way at the end of 1943 and control of assault guns passed to the Panzer arm. Principal users in the Waffen-SS were the seven Panzer divisions which emerged during 1943-44 (Leibstandarte *Adolf Hitler, Das Reich, Totenkopf, Wiking,*

151

Hohenstaufen, Frundsberg and *Hitler Jugend),* and the Panzergrenadier divisions *Polizei, Nordland, Reichsführer-SS, Göt von Berlichingen, Horst Wessel, Nederland* and *Wallonien.* (The main difference between a Panzer and a Panzergrenadier division was that the former had two tank battalions and the latter only one, but conversely a Panzergrenadier division had two infantry regiments and a Panzer division one.) Several Panzergrenadier divisions in fact never received any tanks at all, having to make do with assault guns and tank destroyers which were no real substitute.

After production of the StuG III was interrupted by bombing, a new vehicle entered production at Krupp. This combined the PzKpfw IV chassis with the StuG III superstructure and was known as the StuG IV. It weighed 23 tonnes (22.6 tons), had a top speed of 38 km/h (23.6 mph) and carried 430 l (94.6 gal) of fuel to give a road range of 180 km (112 miles), 120 km (74.5 miles) cross-country. Engine and transmission were the same as in the parent tank and the vehicle's dimensions were length 6.7 m (22 ft), width 2.95 m (9.68 ft), and height 2.2 m (7.22 ft). Frontal armour was thicker than on the StuG III at 80 mm (3.15 in) but the rear was thinner, only 20 mm (0.79 in).

From October 1943, the PzKpfw IV (Ausf F) chassis, engine and transmission were also used as the basis of a new dedicated tank destroyer designed and built by Vomag and designated Jagdpanzer IV. This incorporated further lessons learned from the Russians, who had introduced their own tank destroyer, the SU-85, as an interim way of up-gunning the T-34 until a new turret large enough to accommodate their 85 mm anti-aircraft gun could be built. It featured a completely new superstructure with well-sloped front and sides, the armour protection extending back over the engine deck. A 7.5 cm L/48 weapon was housed frontally in a dome-shaped mantlet. The Jagdpanzer IV weighed 24 tonnes (23.6 tons) and had a road speed of 40 km/h (25 mph). It carried 470 l (103.4 gal) of petrol, giving a road range of 190 km (118 miles), 130 km (81 miles) cross-country. The crew was four men. Overall dimensions of the Jagdpanzer IV were length 6.85 m (22.48 ft), width 3.17 m (10.4 ft), and height

A StuG IV precedes a captured Soviet Su-85 SPG (BA 703/472/20).

1.86 m (6.1 ft), with armour thickness being 60 mm (2.36 in) at the front, 40 mm (1.57 in) on the sides and 30 mm (1.18 in) at the rear.

When sufficient quantities of the 7.5 cm L/70 weapon as fitted to the Panther became available later in 1943 a modified version of this vehicle was so equipped and designated Panzerjäger IV or Jagdpanzer IV (lang). The new gun and an increase in frontal armour to 80 mm (3.15 in) raised the overall weight to 25.8 tonnes (25.39 tons) and performance suffered marginally as a result, speed dropping to 35 km/h (21.75 mph) and both road and cross-country range by 10 km (6 miles). (It is interesting to note that this design was so successful, 1,531 Jagdpanzer IVs of both variants being produced, that an almost identical vehicle has been produced for the modern Bundeswehr designated Jagdpanzer Kanone. It is one of the very few dedicated gun-armed tank destroyers still in production anywhere in the world.)

Another tank destroyer which was built, this time on a composite PzKpfw III/IV chassis, was the

A mounted despatch rider brings a message to the commander of a Nashorn (Hornisse) (BA 278/861/20).

8.8 cm Pak L/71 Hornisse ('Hornet'; an alternative name for the same vehicle was Nashorn — 'Rhinoceros'). Basically this was the same as the Hummel (covered under artillery), with the Maybach HL 120 TRM engine moved from the rear to the front of the vehicle, alongside the driver, but with the long-barrelled 8.8 cm gun instead of the 15 cm field howitzer. Other characteristics, including crew, speed, range and armour, were identical apart from weight, which was 500 kg (1,102.5 lb) greater. The Hornisse formed an important part of the SS Panzer divisions, particularly *Frundsberg*, *Hohenstaufen* and *Hitler Jugend*.

Apart from the PzKpfw III and IV, the chassis of the PzKpfw II and Czech Praga TNHP-S tank (designated PzKpfw 38(t) in German service) were also used as the basis for a variety of tank destroyers. In both cases an open-topped and lightly-armoured superstructure was mounted on the original hull, into which was fitted either a captured Russian 76.2 mm L/54.8 or a 7.5 cm Pak 40 L/46. Vehicles on the PzKpfw II chassis were designated Marder II and those on the PzKpfw 38 (t) Marder III. (There were also a Marder I similarly based upon the French Lorraine tractor chassis but this only saw

Left *A Marder II auf PzKpfw II with 7.5 cm Pak 40 (BA 553/828/24).*

Below *A Marder III auf PzKpfw 38(t) armed with a rebored Russian 7.62 cm gun (BA 218/526/26).*

Below right *Repairs to a 7.5 cm Pak 40 Marder III auf PzKpfw 38(t). Note 'kill' markings on superstructure (BA 241/2167/4).*

second line and training service). Both vehicles had a crew of four and weighed the same, 11.5 tonnes (11.3 tons) with the Russian gun, 10.8 tonnes (10.63 tons) with the Pak 40. The engine in the Marder II was the six-cylinder water-cooled Maybach HL 62 TRM of 6,191 cc which developed 140 bhp at 2,600 rpm giving a top speed of 40 km/h (25 mph) on the heavier vehicle, 55 km/h (34 mph) on the lighter. Power plant in the Czech vehicle was the six-cylinder water-cooled Praga EPA of 7,754 cc which developed 125 bhp at 2,200 rpm giving top speeds of 42-47 km/h (26-29 mph) depending on vehicle weight. The Marder II (76 mm) carried 200 l (44 gal) of petrol, giving a road range of 150 km (93 miles), 100 km (62 miles) cross-country; the 7.5 cm-armed version only carried 170 l (37.4 gal), but because of its lighter weight had the same range. Both versions of the Marder III carried 218 l (48 gal) and had a road range of 240 km (149 miles), 160 km (100 miles) cross-country.

Characteristics of the 76.2 mm Pak 36 (r) and 7.5 cm Pak 40 are given in the section on anti-tank guns under 'Artillery'. Overall dimensions of the four vehicles were as follows. Marder II 76 mm: length 5.65 m (18.54 ft), width 2.3 m (7.55 ft),

and height 2.6 m (8.53 ft); Marder II 7.5 cm: length 4.62 m (15.16 ft), width 2.27 m (7.45 ft), and height 2.2 m (7.22 ft); Marder III 76 mm: length 4.87 m (16 ft), width 2.15 m (7 ft), and height 2.5 m (8.2 ft); Marder III 7.5 cm: length 4.5 m (14.77 ft), width 2.15 m (7 ft), and height 2.4 m (7.88 ft). Armour thickness on the Marder II was 30 mm (1.18 in) frontally, 14.5 mm (0.57 in) on hull sides and rear; on the Marder III it was 50 mm (1.97 in) on the hull front and 10 mm (0.39 in) elsewhere.

Although all four of these vehicles suffered from a rather high profile, and their crews were effectively unprotected against anything heavier than small-arms fire, they gave the anti-tank battalions of the Panzer and Panzergrenadier divisions a useful capability, especially when they could be deployed hull-down in a depression or behind a ridge.

A much more potent tank destroyer on the PzKpfw 38 (t) chassis was the Jagdpanzer 38 (t) Hetzer ('Hunter'); in fact it was so good that it stayed in production in post-war Czechoslovakia and was also manufactured in Switzerland, where it remained in service until the late 1960s! Entering production at the end of 1943, it began to be

issued to the motorized anti-tank battalions in March 1944 and was extremely well-liked by its crews. Weighing 16 tonnes (15.74 tons), it was a low-slung vehicle with extremely well-sloped armour all round mounting the 7.5 cm KwK 42 L/70 as in the Panther. Motive power was the reliable Praga AC/2800 water-cooled petrol engine of 7,754 cc which developed 160 bhp at 2,800 rpm, giving a top speed of 42 km/h (26 mph). Fuel capacity was 320 l (70.4 gal) which gave a road range of 260 km (161 miles), 170 km (106 miles) cross-country.

Crew of the Hetzer was four men and overall dimensions were length 4.87 m (16 ft), width 2.63 m (8.63 ft), and height 2.17 m (7.12 ft). Armour was 60 mm (2.36 in) frontally, 20 mm (0.79 in) elsewhere, but its sharp angles with no shot traps gave a considerable degree of extra protection.

Although the Henschel Tiger I was never converted into a tank destroyer, as mentioned previously the 90 prototype chassis for the VK.4501 produced by Porsche were converted as the Ferdinand or Elefant. This lumbering 68 tonne (66.9 ton) monstrosity mounted the 8.8 cm Pak 43 L/71 in a boxlike superstructure at the rear of the hull, giving it a formidable punch, but to begin with it lacked even a machine-gun for self-protection against infantry and was thus horrifically vulnerable unless well-supported. It was also extremely limited in manoeuvrability: power plant was a pair of Maybach HL 120 TRMS (the same engine as on the PzKpfw IV) which developed only 640 bhp between them at 2,800 rpm, giving a top speed of a mere 20 km/h (12.4 mph). This meant a running infantryman with a limpet mine or satchel of grenades could catch an Elefant with relative ease.

Fuel capacity was 950 l (209 gal) but its engines were so thirsty that the maximum road range was only 130 km (81 miles), and cross-country even worse — 90 km (56 miles). Overall dimensions were length 6.8 m (22.32 ft), width 3.43 m (11.26 ft), and height 2.927 m (9.6 ft). Apart from its gun, later used in the Tiger II, the only redeeming feature of the Elefant was its armour, 200 mm (7.87 in) frontal and 80 mm (3.15 in) at sides and rear, which rendered it more or less invulnerable to enemy tank and anti-tank guns. However, its char-

acteristics made it very much a defensive rather than an offensive weapon and the Elefant suffered badly when first thrown into action at Kursk in July 1943.

The chassis of the Panther and Tiger II were also both used to provide the basis for tank destroyers. The Jagdpanther was unquestionably the finest such vehicle of the war and had been developed as the result of a design requirement dating from October 1942. The first prototype was shown to Hitler on 16 December the following year and production commenced in January 1944. It was a 46 tonne (45.26 ton) vehicle with an extremely well-sloped box superstructure occupying the front of the hull back to the engine louvres, and mounted the same formidable 8.8 cm Pak 43 L/71 gun as the Elefant and Tiger II. Engine, gearbox and so on were the same as the Panther's, but only 700 l (154 gal) of petrol were carried, so range was reduced by 10 km (6 miles).

Dimensions of the four-man Jagdpanther were length 6.87 m (22.55 ft), width 3.27 m (10.73 ft), and height 2.715 m (8.91 ft). Armour protection was 80 mm (3.15 in) frontally and 40-50 mm (1.57-1.97 in) around the sides and rear, so it was even better protected than the Hetzer to which it was almost a 'big brother' in design. If it had gone into production earlier it could have been a far more decisive weapon, but by the time it entered service in the spring of 1944 no quantity of new weapons could save the Reich and in the end only 382 were built.

The same really applies to the Jagdtiger, a tank destroyer on a lengthened Tiger II chassis, but only 74 were produced between 1944 and 1945. This 75 tonne (73.8 ton) monster had a crew of six and mounted the 12.8 cm Pak 44 L/55 which was more than capable of knocking out any tank then or now (other than those fitted with Chobham armour) at ranges well in excess of 1,000 m (1,014 yd) (see 'Artillery' for full description). Unlike the Jagdpanther, it did not have a fully-sloped front plate; instead, a turret-like fixed superstructure was welded to the hull top in between the driver's/radio operator's hatches and the rear engine decking, making it look like a 'tank' even though the 'turret' could not traverse. It was powered by the same

Above *The little Hetzer on PzKpfw 38(t) chassis was a very useful tank destroyer. Its low silhouette can be appreciated when compared with the motor cycle combination (BA 715/213A/25).*

Below *Infantry advance past a disabled Ferdinand or Elefant in Italy (BA 311/940/34).*

Tanks and armoured fighting vehicles

The Jagdpanther was the most effective and deadly tank destroyer of the war. Its clean, well-sloped lines are clearly visible in these three photos (BA 717/17/17, 12 and 20).

Good close-up of a Jagdpanther, probably in southern Russia (BA 721/396/13).

Weapons of the Waffen-SS

engine as the Tiger II (and Panther, far less than half its weight!) and had the same fuel capacity of 860 l (189.2 gal) with the same range, although speed, unsurprisingly, was reduced to 35 km/h (21.75 mph).

Overall dimensions were length 7.8 m (25.6 ft), width 3.625 m (11.9 ft), and height 2.945 m (9.66 ft). It was the most heavily-armoured German vehicle of the war apart from the projected 'Maus' which never entered production, 200-250 mm (7.87-9.84 in) frontally and 80 mm (3.15 in) elsewhere.

*　　*　　*

Apart from these principal AFVs, the various chassis also provided the basis for a variety of specialized vehicles. There were flamethrower versions of the PzKpfw II (1940-42) and III (1942-45); the former had two projectors in the forward part of the hull while the latter had a projector in the turret replacing the gun. Both used compressed nitrogen gas to expel the liquid fuel to a range of some 60 m (197 ft). There were also command (*Befehlswagen*) versions of the PzKpfw II, III, IV and V, usually with dummy guns, the extra space in the turret being occupied with maps and additional radio equipment; and there was a forward observation (*Beobachtungswagen*) version of the PzKpfw III, unarmed apart from a single machine-gun. Finally there were special demolition variants of the PzKpfw IV and Tiger I, the Brummbär ('Grumbler') and the Sturmtiger, the former with a 15 cm howitzer in a fixed superstructure, the latter with a massive 38 cm mortar. Both were designed for assaulting concrete fortifications and for street fighting but they were only produced in tiny quantities and so far as I am aware neither was allocated to any Waffen-SS formation.

Half-tracks, both armoured and unarmoured, also formed the basis for a number of SP anti-tank guns. The ubiquitous SdKfz 251 in particular mounted a variety of different armaments — 3.7, 5 and 7.5 cm Pak and flamethrower — and this and the smaller SdKfz 250 also existed in command, observation, engineer, ambulance and ammunition carrier variants, as well as in the primary role as troop carriers (see following table of variants). The SdKfz 250 was manufactured by Demag from 1940 through to 1944. It weighed 5 tonnes (4.92 tons) empty, 5.7 tonnes (5.6 tons) fully laden with driver, machine-gunner and four men, and was powered by a six-cylinder Maybach HL 42 TRKM water-cooled petrol engine of 4,170 cc which developed 100 bhp at 2,800 rpm to give a top speed of 65 km/h (40 mph). Fuel capacity was 140 l (31 gal), giving a road range of 350 km (217.5 miles), 200 km (124 miles) cross-country. Overall dimensions were length 4.56 m (15 ft), width 1.5 m (6.4 ft), and height (excluding machine-gun shield) 1.66 m (5.45 ft). The armour, which provided protection against shrapnel and small arms fire only, was 12 mm (0.47 in) frontally and 8 mm (0.3 in) at sides and rear. Some 7,500 were built in total.

The SdKfz 251 was the principal vehicle of the Army and SS Panzergrenadier regiments, over 16,000 being built by Hanomag and Borgward. In fact, it was crucial to the Panzer divisions because it allowed the infantry to keep up with the tanks and afforded them some protection while driving into action. It was a 7.4 tonne (7.3 ton) vehicle (8.5 tonnes/8.4 tons fully laden) with a crew of two and capacity for ten men. It first entered service in 1939 and continued in production until late 1944. Power plant was the six-cylinder Maybach HL 42 TUKRM water-cooled petrol engine of 4,170 cc, which developed 100 bhp at 3,000 rpm to give a maximum speed of 52.5 km/h (32.6 mph). The 160 l (35 gal) of fuel carried gave a road range of 320 km (200 miles), 180 km (112 miles) cross-country. Dimensions were length 5.8 m (19 ft), width 2 m (6.56 ft), and height (excluding machine-gun shield) 1.75 m (5.74 ft). Armour protection was identical to that of the SdKfz 250.

SdKfz 251/16 mittlerer Flampanzerwagen Ausf D in action (BA 281/1110/2).

Weapons of the Waffen-SS

SdKfz 250 and 251 variants and production dates

SdKfz 250	Troop carrier	1939-42
SdKfz 250/1	Panzergrenadier vehicle	1942-45
SdKfz 250/2	Telephone vehicle	1940-45
SdKfz 250/3	Radio vehicle (with overhead frame aerial)	1941-45
SdKfz 250/4	Observation vehicle (for artillery)	1943-44
SdKfz 250/5	Mess (kitchen) vehicle	1941-43
SdKfz 250/6	Ammunition carrier	1941-44
SdKfz 250/7	8 cm mortar vehicle	1941-44
SdKfz 250/8	7.5 cm KwK 37 L/24 support vehicle	1943-45
SdKfz 250/9	2 cm KwK 38 L/55 reconnaissance vehicle	1943-44
SdKfz 250/10	3.7 cm Pak L/45 light anti-tank vehicle	1940-42
SdKfz 250/11	2.8 cm sPzB 41 light anti-tank vehicle	1941-43
SdKfz 250/12	Platoon command vehicle	1940-44
SdKfz 252*	Ammunition carrier	1940-41
SdKfz 253*	Observation vehicle	1940-41
SdKfz 251	Troop carrier	1939-44
SdKfz 251/1	28 or 32 cm minelayer (nicknamed 'Stuka on foot'!)	
SdKfz 251/2	8 cm mortar vehicle	
SdKfz 251/3	Radio vehicle (with overhead frame aerial)	
SdKfz 251/4	Ammunition carrier	
SdKfz 251/5	Pioneer (assault engineer) vehicle	
SdKfz 251/6	Commando (infantry assault) vehicle	
SdKfz 251/7	Engineer vehicle (tool carrier)	
SdKfz 251/8	Ambulance	
SdKfz 251/9	7.5 cm StuK 37 L/24 support vehicle	
SdKfz 251/10	3.7 cm Pak L/45 light anti-tank vehicle	
SdKfz 251/11	Telephone vehicle	
SdKfz 251/12	Mess (kitchen) vehicle	
SdKfz 251/13	Sound detector/receiving vehicle	
SdKfz 251/14	Sound detector/recording vehicle	
SdKfz 251/15	Photographic vehicle	
SdKfz 251/16	Flamethrower vehicle	
SdKfz 251/17	2 cm Flak 38 light anti-aircraft vehicle	
SdKfz 251/18	Observation vehicle (for artillery)	
SdKfz 251/19	Radio interception vehicle ('spy truck')	
SdKfz 251/20	Infra-red detection vehicle	
SdKfz 251/21	Triple 1.5 or 2 cm Flak vehicle	
SdKfz 251/22	7.5 cm Pak 40 anti-tank vehicle	

* With metal decking across top of vehicle.

Above left *MG 34 position alongside a knocked-out T-34 which has been turned into the roof of a bunker for the German gunners (BA 83/3380/16a).*

Left *German gunners with a Russian 7.62 cm Model 1941/SiS 3 field gun. This was a hybrid weapon of which few were produced, mounting a Model 1939 barrel with modified recoil mechanism and the addition of a muzzle brake on a 5.7 cm anti-tank gun chassis. In German hands these weapons were designated 7.62 cm FK 288/1(r) (BA 687/134/6a).*

Index

12.8 cm Pak 44 Jagdtiger *136, 156, 161*

Tanks
Production table *111*
PzKpfw I *113*
PzKpfw II *113, 114, 153*; Ausf F *113*;
  Flamm *161*
PzKpfw III *79, 113, 116, 136*; Ausf F
  148; Ausf G *148*; Ausf H *148*; Ausf J
  113, 114, 120, 121, 122, 123; Ausf L
  119, 129; Ausf M *115, 129*; Ausf N
  129; Flamm *161*
PzKpfw IV *106, 113, 114, 133, 136, 152,
  153, 156*; Ausf F1 *122*; Ausf F2 *113,
  122-3, 124*; Ausf G *113, 122, 127,
  129*; Ausf H *128, 129, 147*; Ausf J *129*
PzKpfw V Panther *113, 133, 138, 144,
  153, 156, 161*; Ausf A *136, 139, 141,
  146*; Ausf D *136, 137, 143, 146*; Ausf
  G *136, 137, 143, 146*
PzKpfw VI Tiger I *86, 107, 113, 123,
  129, 130, 131, 132, 133, 134, 135,
  137, 147, 156, 161*
PzKpfw VI Tiger II *113, 133, 135, 136,
  147, 148, 156, 161*
PzKpfw 38(t) *153*

Units
1st Panzer Div *146*
1st SS Standarte *8-9*
5th SS Panzer Regt *147*
5th SS Sturm Brigade *62, 83*
7th 'Ghost' Panzer Div *86*
8th Panzer Div *102*
Afrika Korps *113*
Charlemagne, 33rd SS Div *41*
Condor Legion 78-9
Das Reich, 2nd SS Div *7, 43, 54, 110,
  135, 151*
Dirlewanger 'Division' *37*
Der Führer Regt *7, 20*
Deutschland Regt *7*
Frundsberg, 10th SS Div *152, 153*
Germania Regt *7*
Götz von Berlichingen, 17th SS Div *152*
Großdeutschland Div *135*
Handschar, 13th SS Div *46, 71*
Hermann Göring, Luftwaffe Div *60*
Hitler Jugend, 12th SS Div *152, 153*
Hohenstaufen, 9th SS Div *151, 153*
Horst Wessel, 18th SS Div *152*
Karstjäger, 24th SS Div *46, 71*
Leibstandarte *Adolf Hitler*, 1st SS Div *7,
  14, 71, 110, 135, 146, 151*

Nederland, 23rd SS Div *152*
Nord, 6th SS Div *46, 71*
Nordland Regt *40*
Division *135, 152*
Panzer Lehr Div *135*
Prinz Eugen, 7th SSDiv *7, 20, 23, 44,
  46, 71, 152*
Polizei, 4th SS Div *71, 152*
Reichsführer-SS, 16th SS Div *152*
schwere Pz Abt 501-510 *134*
schwere SS Pz Abt 101 *129, 134, 148*
schwere SS Pz Abt 102 and 103 *134, 148*
schwere SS Pz Abt 501 and 502 *148*
schwere SS Pz Abt 503 *135, 148*
Skanderberg, 21st SS Div *46, 71*
SS-VT *7, 14, 71*
Stabswache *7, 10*
Totenkopf, 3rd SS Div *7, 71, 110, 127,
  135, 151*
Totenkopfverbände *7*
Ungarische Nr 1 and 2, 25th and 26th SS
  Divs *40*
Verfügungsdivision — see SS-VT
Wallonien Legion *14, 45*
Wallonien, 28th SS Div *83, 152*
Wiking, 5th SS Div *7, 40, 104, 110, 120,
  147, 151*